A Cauldron of Anxiety

Capitalism in the twenty-first century

A Cauldron
of Anxiety

Capitalism in the twenty-first century

William Briggs

Winchester, UK
Washington, USA

JOHN HUNT PUBLISHING

First published by Zero Books, 2021
Zero Books is an imprint of John Hunt Publishing Ltd., No. 3 East St., Alresford,
Hampshire SO24 9EE, UK
office@jhpbooks.com
www.johnhuntpublishing.com
www.zero-books.net

For distributor details and how to order please visit the 'Ordering' section on our website.

ISBN: 978 1 78904 609 0
978 1 78904 610 6 (ebook)
Library of Congress Control Number: 2020934417

A CIP catalogue record for this book is available from the British Library.

Design: Stuart Davies

UK: Printed and bound by CPI Group (UK) Ltd, Croydon, CR0 4YY
Printed in North America by CPI GPS partners

We operate a distinctive and ethical publishing philosophy in
all areas of our business, from our global network of authors to
production and worldwide distribution.

Contents

Also by William Briggs

Classical Marxism in an Age of Capitalist Crisis: the past is prologue, Routledge, ISBN: 978-1-13834-428-0
Removing the Stalin Stain, Zero Books, ISBN: 978-1-78904-521-5

For those who have always known that there is a
better way
and especially for Rose

Introduction

There is a real and present danger facing our world. Its name is capitalism and the danger lies in the simple but inescapable fact that capitalism is now well past its use-by date. Ours has become a world of intense anxiety, fear and alienation and it is taking a real toll on the people. These fears might appear to be localised; will my job last, will I be able to pay that bill, will my children be safe, and will they have a future? The fears might be global; will there be war, will the planet be consumed by climate change?

The existence of capitalism has always meant that people have been forced to struggle to survive. However, today we are experiencing acute levels of poverty, distress, homelessness, mental illness. To put it simply; capitalism is making us and the planet upon which we live, sick. Capitalism had a beginning, a middle and is approaching its end. It appears not to be prepared to go gently into any good night any time soon, but it is, as Trotsky described so clearly, in its death agony. This long and overdue death inevitably means a lot of misery for the people.

We are, in the main, an optimistic species. To be otherwise would be disastrous. No matter how bad things might be, there is always a light shining, if sometimes dimly, on the horizon. Things will get better. The problem is that capitalism's crisis, and the crisis that we all feel as a consequence, makes it harder and harder to be optimistic, or more accurately, have any belief that capitalism has any answers to our collective woes. In the face of utter hopelessness, Roberto, the hapless Italian migrant, in the 1986 film *Down by Law*, maintained an irrepressible optimism. He was in a US prison. He had been charged with murder. He had little English and nobody to support him. Life was conspiring against him. He appeared to have no chance. Despite all this he would repeat, and repeat again, a line that he had heard and committed to memory. "It's a sad and beautiful world." Well Roberto, the world has become a lot sadder and its beauty has dimmed. Roberto's take on things may well be just about the greatest overestimation that any of us will ever hear or read. The facts just seem to speak for themselves.

The horizon is low, there is a bleakness, and a sense of helplessness and hopelessness hangs in the air. There is more accumulated wealth on the planet than there has ever been, and yet fewer and fewer people enjoy the fruits of that wealth. According to the latest estimates, global wealth now stands at $360 trillion, and just 26 individuals have as much wealth as 3.8 billion people on the planet. Perhaps they are better managers, more astute than you or me, but something doesn't seem quite right. They are statistics that simply defy logic, that are impossible to imagine. What is easier to get your head around is the simple fact that we live in a world where inequality is growing at the same rate that wealth becomes concentrated into the hands of a shrinking but indecently rich few. For the vast majority life is a struggle. It is becoming a world once only written about by sci-fi writers, the dystopian future scenario. It is a world where ideas are censored, journalists are threatened and, as in the case of Julian Assange, threatened with a lifetime in prison. For what? For exposing war crimes. It is a world of globalising capitalism and of trade wars. It is a world where the threat of war hangs over us. It is a world of climate change and potential catastrophe. It short, it is a world of fear and alienation, where thought is to be manipulated and questioning to be mistrusted. Welcome to the world of late capitalism, a time of barbarity. It is a difficult time to be alive. But it need not be so. Humanity, unchained from alienation and fear, has the capacity to soar. This book sets itself a task. In the face of such a miserable checklist, it sets about explaining how things got to this stage and how it can be changed. Surely that is not too big a task.

Not another self-help book

There are times when even the most stoic amongst us can feel a little estranged and alienated from the world and from life. If you are ever feeling down, confused, overwhelmed by all that life throws at you; money, stress, work, unemployment, self-image, self-worth, the state of the world, climate change, urban infrastructure, commuting times, racism, aged care, youth care, rising suicide rates, sexism, anxiety, sleep deprivation, depression, housing affordability, homelessness, drug use, sexual violence, job insecurity, national security, refugees, or the threat of war, then there is a book within easy reach and available at any good bookshop, or on-line, at airport news-stands, in most news agencies, or advertised and discussed on television talk shows. There will be a book that seems to be written just for you and specially designed to help you. These books exist and proliferate because we are drowning in a sea of anxiety and fear. The fears are all real and the books that roll endlessly off the presses do, just occasionally, offer some sound advice, but more often just alert the reader to even more anxieties and fears. It is impossible to ignore the tsunami of self-help literature. The good people at Amazon, in the spirit of the times, and doubtless in an attempt at "helping" either us or possibly themselves, have broken the self-help genre into 28 sub-sections, so take heart, there is something for everyone.

The self-help authors respond to problems that exist, but the reader is unlikely to be better off for the experience of that one special book. The authors are good at isolating problems but are less well-equipped at explaining how the problem arose, where it came from, and what we can do, as a society, to remove the problem, and rarely link one problem with another. Diagnosis is fine but simply treating symptoms is not what is required.

Opinion shapers, the media, pollsters and survey-takers are sometimes even worse. The opinion pollster is very good at providing short lists, from which we are asked to choose, or place the issues we are catastrophising about in some order of "preference". We all know the format. A list is presented, in no special order. You are then asked to pick from the list. Every item, which is never exhaustive, is a blight. The responses show us and the world what the problems are. Choosing the worst three becomes a subjective affair and can potentially drive you off to the self-help shelves again.

On any given day, we will find the media focusing on some of these problems. Well-meaning and earnest experts will be rounded up and suitably sage advice will be given as to the best way of "fixing" the nominated problem. There is an inevitability about how all this will play out. To be absolutely fair, sometimes, just occasionally, a problem might be sorted, but the bigger the problem the less likely will it be that a happy ending will be the end-result.

Now, don't get me wrong. We all need help, especially as the society we live in has cut us all loose and there are no safeguards and no sureties and only the strongest can expect to survive, let alone thrive. Here we all are, anxious, fearful and alienated. Perhaps what we need is a self-help book. Don't be alarmed. This is not another "self-help" book, well not in the strictest sense of the word. It might be classified as a "collective-health" book but is unlikely to be listed by Amazon as the twenty-ninth category. The term is only used to point out that the atomisation, the individualisation of society, has left us alone and isolated, and that's not the way we come, or are meant to be. A thousand self-help books aimed at a thousand individualised disorders can only make for more isolation and alienation. Such a book as this, on the other hand, identifies a common denominator. That common denominator is capitalism and the rule of capital. Just about every problem that keeps you awake at night is caused by capitalism. If we can recognise that simple truth, then "help" is possible.

This is a book about how society works or doesn't work in our interests. It is about how we have come to be swirling helplessly around in this cauldron of anxiety, fear and alienation. It is about how we might find our way to shore, to a safe harbour and to recognise that life just doesn't have to be like this. It is a book about another way of organising lives and society. It is about a future that is worth considering and striving for. It's about Marxism. It's about socialism.

Unfortunately, these two words have become loaded. There is still a perception that Marxism is almost up there with devil worship. To use the term is to bring down the wrath of every decent conservative political thinker and to be fair, the term has been badly abused, not just by those same decent conservatives but by a raft of those on the left. We have those who cling to the lie that Marxism somehow equates to Stalinism. The problem is then compounded when just about anything that can be critiqued is critiqued and has the tag "Marxist" either applied to it or is self-applied. There are many Marxist schools of thought, Marxist analyses of just about everything and in just about every area of physical or mental endeavour. Marxist critiques flourish, not only of capitalism but of other Marxist theories. There are a dizzying array of texts, conferences, papers and commentaries from legions of ever more shrill and discordant Marxist thinkers and writers. Sorting through all of this is no easy task, and you might be pleased to learn that I am not about to wade through the polemics and struggles between "Marxist" schools. I will defend Marxism and socialism but by contrasting it to what passes for the "best imaginable" system; capitalist democracy.

We have been told and told again, from generation to generation, that our system, while "flawed", is the best of all possible systems in the best of all possible worlds. After a time, the slogans become the truth, or at least a fog of incomprehension descends. Aldous Huxley, in his *Brave New World*, wrote that, "A really efficient totalitarian state would be one in which the all-powerful executive of political bosses and their army of managers control a population of slaves who do not have to be coerced, because they love their servitude." His book was used to argue against the authoritarian state. It became a "teachable" moment in the battle of ideas against the USSR. It has a powerful message. It is an echo of two other ideas that were presented by Marxists in two different eras. Friedrich Engels used the sometimes maligned but accurate term "false consciousness" to describe a situation whereby the ideas of the ruling class are taken on, willingly, by the working class. Antagonisms between the classes become increasingly masked until they "seem" to vanish. We end up with a situation where the unemployed, the impoverished, the homeless, still maintain that their interests are the same as those running the system that has made them unemployed, poor and homeless. This idea of Engels was adapted, only marginally, by Italian Marxist Antonio Gramsci and re-badged as cultural hegemony. Put simply, power is maintained by a combination of economic power and state power. The effectiveness of state control and its ability to evoke a feeling, not merely of acceptance, but of willing acceptance on the part of the working class has been, by any measure, extraordinarily successful.

Huxley's attack on totalitarianism was rather like George Orwell's in *Animal Farm*. For him, a means to successfully controlling thoughts and actions was through simple slogans, and the simpler, the better. Orwell's "four legs good, two legs bad" can be translated to any nationalist slogan from any country. Calls to protect borders, warnings that foreigners are taking our jobs, that we can make America, or Australia, or Britain, or anywhere else on the planet "great again" are no better or worse than Orwell's quick-fix slogans.

The point here is that we need to remember that those who make the rules tend to dominate the thinking of a society. It is an idea that sits at the heart of Marxist criticisms of capitalist rule. So, when we hear that Marxism or socialism is anti-people, anti-societal, that it is against the best interests of us all, then perhaps we might pause just for a moment and repeat (silently of course) "four legs good, two legs bad" in the way of an affirming mantra. Mantras, however, while certainly having their place, are notoriously ineffective at changing widely held opinions. The state, as the organiser of capitalist rule, has very cleverly and over a period of generations, managed to ensure that these widely held opinions don't change. If things get a little prickly, if inequality rises appreciably, if the system does not provide as it was supposed to, then it is important to limit and mute voices of opposition. It makes sense to hive people off into groups and sub-groups. We might be permitted to protest about this policy, or that injustice, support this cause, engage in the politics of identity, struggle for the politics of gender, sexuality, race, ethnicity, or whatever, and at the end of the day just possibly achieve some small victory but without changing anything of real substance. We are certainly not encouraged to have long memories, or to read widely. We are actively discouraged from "joining up the dots". The fact is that every issue that troubles us is linked to every other issue, but it is safer to keep us ignorant of this simple fact. Huxley's recipe for a successful totalitarian rule remains true today. The same apparatus that has made Marxism a dirty word has also dulled our collective capacities for remembrance and thought. Ray Bradbury in *Farenheit 451* reminded the world that book burning was little more than a symbolic act. The books, he explained, are first figuratively burned by us. We don't have to physically burn books, just ignore them and then content ourselves with less depth and analysis in our news and before you know it, we have arrived at ground zero. Ideas are, of course, worrying and dangerous things. As Fire Chief Beatty explains in Bradbury's book, "if you don't want a man unhappy politically, don't give him two sides to a question to worry him; give him one. Better yet, give him none."

Ideas and focus

This book is a gentle reminder of those warnings. It is a book about big ideas but does not pretend to be a "big" book. The major authors that I shall refer to in this book (Marx, Engels, Lenin, Trotsky) wrote big books and had big ideas. They are ideas that are worth returning to and worth defending. They answered some big questions when they were written, and the answers are even more prescient today than when they were first written and first read. They are the dangerous ideas that could change the world and change it for the better. They are the words that framed what we know as Marxism.

Marxism has two closely interrelated objectives. It seeks to explain the world and after answering the questions of why things are as they are, it seeks to change the world. After all, if this much maligned philosophy existed merely to point an accusing finger and to expose what was wrong, and not offer a guide to action, then it becomes all rather pointless. None of us want to waste our time. However, even if Marxism did only act in an explanatory way, it would have earned a well-deserved place in history. Remember that list of fears and anxieties? Marxist analysis joins up the dots. Understanding things can be a source of comfort and power. We are less obviously adrift and subject to the ebbs and flows of an otherwise inexplicable current.

The book, then, sets out to "do" a number of things. Its first task is to offer a brief overview of just what Marxism is and what it is for and to explain what capitalism is all about. It next explains how we got to the parlous state in which we find ourselves. From here we isolate some of the key issues facing the world; some of the worrying, sleep-depriving things that have become a gravy-train for the self-help authors. A Marxist perspective allows us to understand and explain how these problems arose, how they proliferated and how they can be resolved.

The work begins in chapter 1 by looking at the question "how did we end up here?" It offers a brief outline of what capitalism is, how it operates, and of the contradictions that have both acted to move it forward and now act to destroy it. The chapter also describes the state and its role as a facilitator of capitalist relations before focusing on the question of how it is that capitalism has managed to survive.

The theme of alienation in society and of how capitalism and alienation are inseparable is taken up in chapter 2. It is a theme that runs through the book. Marx's conception of alienation in the workplace is discussed as is the deepening sense of loss of individuality and self that we are experiencing in this century as capitalism has commodified everything, not least the individual. This idea is taken a step further in chapter 3, which expands on the idea of alienation as it has come to affect political responses to capitalist rule. In particular the chapter discusses the rise of identity politics as opposed to the politics of class and how identity politics grew as an intensifying crisis in capitalism became more evident. The fact that the state appears to accept identity politics as a "proof" that the system works is rather significant.

Chapter 4 takes, as its starting point, the rise of populist political movements as a response to the crisis that is besetting the world and how populism, in turn, is being used by the state to seek to restore a sense of legitimacy to political structures that are enjoying less and less support. Along with populist politics sits economic nationalism, the politics of trade wars, and a rise in nationalism. This rise in nationalist sentiment, in turn, can only serve to increase fears and anxieties as blame for a failing system is laid at the feet of the "other" and not at the door of the real culprit – a failing capitalist economic and political system. Chapter 5 briefly deals with the "crisis" year of 2019. It was a time of incredible upheavals across continents as well as an intensification of labour unrest in developed economies that have not been seen for decades. The chapter asks why, at this point in history, is this occurring and offers a Marxist response; that the economic formation that is capitalism has reached a point where it has nothing more to offer, and like economic formations that have preceded it, is ready to be replaced by something better and more rational.

Our world is facing what can only be described as existential crises. Chapter 6 describes these crises; the drive to war that is imminent but not necessarily inevitable and the climate crisis that is engulfing the planet. These two issues are of terrifying enormity. As capitalism tears itself apart it also threatens to tear the world apart. Trade wars have become the norm and the threat of global war has never been higher. The crisis of climate change is the crisis of capitalism. The devastation that we are witnessing is real and is having a devastating impact on the health of the planet and on the mental health of countless millions of people who seek responses and are so often made to feel a personal and collective guilt for the crimes of capitalism.

Chapter 7 asks a final question. What is to be done? It is a question that needs to be asked but more importantly needs to be answered. The book promotes Marxism as a means of challenging capitalism and therefore overcoming the fear, anxiety and alienation that goes with capitalism. The chapter offers an optimistic view of the future, or at least presents a way that can lead to optimism.

Ultimately this is not a book about theory, although political theory is absolutely central to what will be discussed. It does not set itself the task of discussing in fine detail the whys and wherefores of Marxist theory, of how theory became detached from practice, or of the bitter debates and divisions that have been so much a part of Marxist history. Rather it uses the words of Marx and his co-thinkers to make sense of what is happening in our world.

Marx's words and ideas are eminently accessible. He and his fellow theorists were writing, not for an academic market, not to bedazzle the reader with scholarly language that becomes more obtuse and more impenetrable with each passing decade. Marx and his comrades were writing for working men and women. It is little wonder then that one little book, the *Manifesto of the Communist Party*, is still in print 170 years after first making its appearance, has been sold to millions upon millions of people around the world, and is read in 200 languages. It evokes a feeling of optimism and Marxism and Marxists remain optimistic about the future.

Marxism and socialism are polar opposites of capitalism. The state and its various institutions have laboured long and hard to convince us that capitalist democracy and the economic system that goes with it are as good as it gets. When considered against the backdrop of a fractured society, growing inequality and despair, and with no hope in sight, then that does not seem to be much of an endorsement. Despite this obvious problem, to seriously question whether such a system has the right to continue is still regarded by many as something akin to heresy. The fact is that life continues to get harder, bleaker and more difficult for more and more people. People are slowly being driven to madness as we wade through the veritable swamp of fear and loathing that capitalism has given us up to. It is high time that we left that swamp and looked to something better.

Chapter 1

How did we end up here?

It doesn't need a lot of analytical skill to recognise that things are in rather poor shape. We hear and read that fewer people are engaging with the media, or at least with what passes for traditional media, to keep informed. The same can be said for engagement with the political process. There is something of an irony here, or rather a sense of worry is becoming very pronounced on the part of many an opinion-moulder in our midst. Writers, commentators and more than the occasional politician express concern about this sorry state of affairs. Opinion-pieces appear with gay abandon, and knowledgeable fingers are wagged at the degree of disengagement and apathy that is so evident. All seek answers and publish their answers, to be read by an audience that some might unkindly refer to as the "chattering classes". The articles are read, heads shake, tongues cluck, knowing sighs are sighed, and the "astute" reader knows that he or she is wise. It is those "others" who have broken the sacred covenant and are turning away from the verities. Cue publishing deals. The articles are gathered together, to become chapters in books that prove to the faithful that a tweak here, or a shuffle there will fix things. We are reminded on an almost daily basis that there is nothing fundamentally wrong with the system and that in any case there is absolutely no alternative but to make it work. While all of this goes on, the people whose lives are most affected by the day-to-day grind and alienation ignore the experts and retreat further from an engagement that appears to not serve their interests.

It is hard to feel judgemental about this. We have a population bombarded with trivia and ever more truncated news. The news becomes depressing and confusing. There is a sense of unreality. If your primary concern is how you might stretch a shrinking budget a little further, or if you will have enough hours of paid employment to keep a roof over your head, then it is easy to either dismiss reports of global threats or to simply line up with the latest anti-China, anti-Russia, anti-refugee, or anti-whomever tirade. Many are swayed, as they have been for decades, by such short, easy to digest explanations as to why things are bad. Others simply put up the shutters. Those who have created the problem go about their business and remain unchallenged. Nobody seems to want to look for the real culprit.

Capitalism and the state have worked closely for a long time to make sure that there is a sense of harmony and that the people accept that all is as it should be. Marxists, on the other hand, point out that under the surface there is a reality marked by antagonisms that centre around class and exploitation. It has been this way ever since capitalism, as we recognise it, developed during the industrial revolution. One of the more dangerous things that our guardians, the "keepers of the keys", might have to contend with is memory. The shorter the memory, the better. Our collective memory is becoming shorter. If we look at any developed economy and cast back 50 years, we can see a whole lot of things, once the accepted norms, not only shattered but all but forgotten. Living standards were growing, there was a belief that children would inherit a better life than that of their parents, that health outcomes would continue to improve, that public infrastructure would get progressively better, that the working week would shorten, that education was intrinsically valuable and not tied to a dollar value. The economy was either stable or growing. It was a period that has been described as the "golden age" of capitalism. Admittedly this was but a fleeting time, from the end of WWII until the early 1970s, but even these memories are fading ones. Capitalism is returning to the avaricious and all devouring creature that it always was. Reading Dickens, today, is less fiction and more journalism.

So, how did we get here? Something has clearly gone very wrong. Why is life so hard for so many? To understand this, it is necessary to first understand capitalism, its development, how it works and for whom. Those whose task it is to promote the system are unlikely to offer much by way of answers. Every time another crack appears in the economic structure, a queue of "experts" will form to trot out well-worn clichés. There are "headwinds", the "fundamentals are sound", it is just a "correction", "our economy is the envy of the world". The slogans are repeated, and repeated again, while fewer and fewer listen to them and nobody seems to have the armoury or the will to do anything about it. Capitalism, we are told, is the best option, no, the only option. Parliamentary democracy safeguards our rights and freedoms. They are repeated until no alternative can be uttered or even considered. If something goes wrong, if there is a recession, or a corruption scandal, or banks behave badly, it is the fault of this or that individual, or we are reassured that the system can self-correct. Have no fear, all is well. If you feel the government to be not acting in your best interests, then get rid of them at the ballot box. A new government will fix the problem. In the deep recesses of our consciousness we all know this is foolish talk, but the great heresy once articulated by Marx and later paraphrased by Lenin remains that, "the oppressed are allowed once every few years to decide which particular representatives of the oppressing class shall represent and repress them in parliament" (Lenin 1977: 270).

Only a very few years ago such a sentiment as that expressed by Marx more than a century ago would have been considered ludicrous. Political parties enjoyed the support of the bulk of the population. The term "rusted" on had not been coined, but it well-described the feelings of people. Membership of mainstream political parties was high and there was a feeling (rightly or wrongly) that parliamentary politics meant something and that there were real differences between parties, because they dealt in ideas. Now, just as is the case with a general disengagement with the media, there is a disengagement with the political process and especially in what is best described as "bourgeois" political processes. Something is obviously wrong. The state needs us to remain on-side. How long apathy will equate to acceptance is another matter.

So, if something has gone wrong, and capitalism is not providing the answers, a few questions need to be asked. How did capitalism become the only game in town? How did it develop? Why is it always either in crisis or about to slip into crisis? What makes it tick and how does it keep going?

What is capitalism?

So, what is this crisis-ridden economic and political system that determines our lives, this "machine" that we call capitalism? Where did it spring from, how does it work and why is it the problem, the cause of our fear and distress? A definition is as good a place to start as any. There are many to choose from, but this does the job nicely. "Pure capitalism is defined as a system wherein all of the means of production (physical capital) are privately owned and run by the capitalist class for a profit, while most other people are workers who work for a salary or wage (and who do not own the capital or the product)" (Zimbalist and Sherman 1984: 6-7). As an economic system, this format has been most successful. It has created vast wealth and in its early days revolutionised the way people lived and worked. The fact of the matter is, however, that it did not always exist. It broke apart the old feudal way of life and offered enormous potential. It was an idea whose time had come. It had to be. It built the nation-state as we recognise it today and globalised the world economy. The history of the world is a long one and we can but hope that humanity has a long future. Capitalism should not be expected to be some eternal, immutable system. This, however, is not the way it is perceived by many adherents of the system and is certainly not the way that it is presented to us by those who run things. It came into being because feudalism had reached its use-by date. Feudalism had been a step forward from slavery but no longer had anything to offer. Capitalism did offer much and provided much, but if it becomes regressive, then it is time for something to change. Capitalism's day in the sun, just as feudalism and slavery before that, is over.

Just as that truth becomes so abundantly clear, the salutes and tributes to capitalism become louder and more strident. Some have an almost messianic zeal. "Thanks to capitalism, Americans as a nation are living dramatically better and longer than they did at the beginning of the twentieth century" (Forbes and Ames: 2009). Writing such a book, just a year after the Great Financial Crisis of 2008, was a brave action, an act of faith, but more than a little ridiculous.

In 2005, Alan Greenspan, at the time the Chairman of the Federal Reserve of the US, remarked that "the income gap between the rich and the rest of the US population has become so wide, and is growing so fast, that it might eventually threaten the stability of democratic capitalism itself" (Christian Science Monitor 2005). The zealots might argue that they are talking in general trend terms but, as Robert Gordon (2016) shows, the United States has entered a period of permanent economic stagnation that will be marked above all by growing social inequality and poverty. Replace the term United States for just about any capitalist country and the story reads the same. Greenspan was writing in 2005, Gordon, in 2016. Have they been proven right or wrong? How do things look today?

It seems that the deeper into the mire that capitalism slips, the more ringing are the claims that all in the garden is rosy. I once had a cat. They can be funny creatures. Whenever he mistook a leap or took a tumble, he would stand, stock-still, pause and then purposefully lick his shoulder, almost as if to say, "it's no big deal". When the shrill voices supporting capitalism, as it stumbles from crisis to crisis, proclaim its beauty, I am reminded of my cat. While it's nice to reminisce, my sympathies do not go out to the shoulder licking apologists for capitalism.

Capitalism then, is an economic and political system in which a country's trade and industry are controlled by private owners for profit, rather than by the state, let alone the people. It's a neat, tidy and simple description. It almost has a benign ring to it. Capitalism is said to reward hard work, to offer opportunities, to eradicate poverty and to free the human spirit. But there is another capitalism. It is the one that countless millions of ordinary people live with on a daily basis. But capitalism is not some Jekyll and Hyde creature. There is only Hyde. Capitalism's existence is predicated on profit. Profit can only come from labour. This means a division of society along lines of class. Production is from labour, which is social in nature. Profits are taken which are private in nature. We have the beginning of a series of contradictions. Capitalism is competitive. Wealth inevitably becomes concentrated into fewer and fewer hands. The economic cycle is marked by booms and busts, crisis follows crisis and the losers are inevitably the ones who created the wealth in the first place. Capitalism must exploit. It's just how things are. It also must expand.

Marx and Engels famously stated that "the need of a constantly expanding market for its products chases the bourgeoisie over the whole surface of the globe. It must nestle everywhere, settle everywhere, establish connexions everywhere" (1977: 39). Whether this is inherently good or bad depends to an extent on how you wish to view the logic of capitalism. It is also dependent on where capitalism sits on its historical time-line. On its path to maturity, capitalism certainly revolutionised the way things worked and how things were organised. It changed reality not only in the countries of Europe, from whence the system first emerged, but increasingly across the globe.

Capitalism changed the world and all human relationships.

This is inevitably linked to its capacity for exploitation and expansion. If we start with a small example, we can see how things move towards a global economy. Capitalism began in a small way in a relatively localised setting and could not help but move beyond the local, to the national and to what we see today; an increasingly integrated global economy. How? Human ingenuity played a huge role. Imagine that we are living in an age that coincides with the beginning of capitalism. You have an idea. You see around you a good natural resource – wool. People in the community have been spinning and weaving for their own use and for neighbours for as long as anyone cares to remember. You set up a slightly more efficient spinning operation and with the labour of a few local people begin making woollen coats. They sell well. The local market is soon saturated. You then move into a bigger market, employ more people and become more wealthy as a result. The regional market is flooded. On the other side of the country there is another coat-maker. You make your operation bigger, more productive, employ better looms and find that your product can undersell the competitor. You achieve success, but again the bigger market becomes flooded. To survive, you must find new markets, diversify your product and expand. Profitability becomes tricky. You cut wages if possible, use better technology and expand into neighbouring countries. You overcome the problem, for a time, but other producers in other countries are doing the same thing. There is a clash of interests. You call on the state to support you. After all you are providing employment for a great many people. You are a good corporate citizen. Everybody is relying on you to keep going and growing. The state supports you and puts tariffs on foreign coats that might undersell yours. Your position is saved, your wealth grows, at least for a time. This is replicated hundreds of times over until we see capitalism expanding as a global entity.

Some rather significant things flow from this example. The first is that not one coat could have been sold, and not one dollar of profit could have been reaped without the labour of the workers who spun the wool, who operated the looms, who cut the cloth and made the coat. Their labour is the single most important element in this capitalist equation. They are paid for their labour, but the profit comes from this labour. In Marxist terms this is known as surplus value and is the source of all capital. While the worker may be said to "freely" enter into this relationship, it is always tilted toward the coercive end of the scale.

The idea of surplus value and capital's absolute reliance on surplus value sits at the heart of Marxist economic theory. How it works is simple enough. Let us say that the worker is paid $30 per hour operating a machine that produces components for that rather stylish woollen coat. Now, let us imagine that this worker is able to turn out $120 worth of product in an hour. The employer's costs might add up to an additional $30, for plant and equipment. So, for an outlay of $60, the employer ends up with a surplus of $60, a surplus value of $60. The worker sells his or her capacity to work and is paid for only a proportion of that labour. Surplus value, therefore, becomes the source of all profit. This might sound simplistic, but it rather accurately describes the process as it existed when Marx was writing and is in no way changed today. Without labour there is no product, no profit, no capital growth, no capitalist system.

Workers have traditionally sought to combine with other workers to advance their interests. These interests included, and still do, getting a greater slice of the pie, a decent life and a chance to enjoy a life apart from a life that is labour. The interests of the working class are opposed to those of the employer or ruling class. A clash of interests can only be avoided by a range of state institutions becoming involved. These have invariably been placed at the convenience of the employer. There were, of course, institutions that were established by the workers themselves, and the most obvious of these are the trade unions.

While the unions remain potentially powerful organisations, it remains a fact that, over time, they have been integrated into the broader state institutions and are no longer independent of the state.

The state and capitalism enjoy a symbiotic relationship. Each needs the other. The two have developed alongside one another. The state facilitates capitalist development. After all it is a state of the dominant idea and capitalism is that dominant idea. Our simple example of the coat-manufacturer ended with the state acting to protect the industry. This has had a history of difficulties. Capitalist production and relationships become a global affair and yet the nation-state is called upon to protect local capital. The lead up to WWI was set against just such a crisis of capitalist development and national response. Trade war and currency war politics seem to show that little has been learned.

How people live and how they interrelate and interact is bound up with the development of capitalism. The way goods are produced reflects the social nature of humanity. Production is a social activity. This is contradicted by the private nature of ownership. This is but one of the contradictions that go, hand in hand, with capitalism. It is a contradiction that has a connection to the way we live today – in that sea of fear and loathing and in a cauldron of anxiety and alienation.

How it works – contradictions

Capitalism has, from its first moment, been enmeshed in irresolvable contradictions. This is a curious feature of the beast and is, I suppose, yet one more contradiction. Each of these contradictions is potentially life-threatening for capitalism. Taken as a whole, they pose a real and present danger. It has sought to escape them but without success. They have at once promoted capitalism's forward motion while, over time, have become deeper and more acute.

First among these contradictions is the private ownership of the means of production and the social nature of the production process. This has remained unsolvable precisely because capitalism requires classes – an exploiting and exploited class. Their needs are always different and always antagonistic.

Next is the need of capitalism to maximise profit by expanding the productive processes and surplus value, which means, among other things, limiting real wages growth. If an individual capitalist enterprise does not grow, then it is swallowed up by another or simply fades away into obscurity. The same logic can be said to apply to the whole system.

The third flows directly from the second. The absolute need to increase labour productivity contributes to a tendency for overall profit rates to fall. If this is permitted, then disaster follows and yet it is always there, lurking in the shadows. Capitalism only survives if profitability continues to grow. This worrisome aspect of life for capitalism has compelled it to globalise its production and increasingly to integrate operations across states and continents. The final and potentially devastating contradiction is in this inescapable drive to a globalised economy while relying on the nation-state system to administer capitalist relations. The term "potentially devastating" is used not from a desire to be theatrical, but is based on a logical premise. Nation-states and globalised capital do not and cannot have identical agendas, even if the state exists to facilitate capitalism. We have seen this turn rather ugly when in 1914, this fundamental contradiction erupted into global war. Trade wars and currency wars are unwinnable. We all know that. Despite this knowledge, they can and have in the past taken a further step into the abyss.

Even if that can be avoided, we are left with the environmental devastation that is continuing. We need to remember who has created the mess that we find ourselves in. Climate change is a direct result of capitalism and yet capitalism is rarely held accountable. It is no secret that just 100 global capitalist corporations account for over 70 per cent of global carbon emissions (Griffith 2017) and yet we are made to feel individual responsibility. The people are made to feel personal guilt, rather than seeing themselves as victims of destructive capitalist processes. In other words, capitalism, not the people, is the guilty party. Capitalism has brought the planet to the brink. It is not the people that are driven to return increasing profits, or who must out-perform rivals, find bigger markets and newer ways of extracting resources.

The act of running from, or outpacing, contradictions that might well consume the system did, in truth, serve capitalism well in happier days. Each problem, although it could never be overcome, could be used to further promote growth and expansion. The perpetually nagging problem of the potential for profit rates to fall is a prime example. The rate of profit in Marx's work is defined as the ratio of profit to investment. Over time this ratio becomes problematic. Greater investment does not necessarily equate to an equally high return and so there is a tendency for the rate of profit to begin to slide. This need not run along anything like a convenient straight path. The rate rises and falls but there is always the danger of that very tendency to become a major threat. This becomes especially evident when down-turns or crises in the economy occur. They have, as we are painfully aware, been occurring more and more frequently. This feature of the economy is described in detail by Marx (*Capital Vol. 3* 1986: 211-231). This "difficulty" becomes a key factor in the drive to globalisation. Among a range of options that capital can employ to remove such an obstacle, or at least to postpone and forestall the worst outcomes, is to continually expand and to internationalise its relations. This means, in effect, a continual motion and an endless battle to survive. This inherent contradiction between the need to expand and the tendency for falling rates of profit has been and remains central to globalisation.

The problem for capitalism, and by implication the problem for all of us who must live in the dysfunctional world of capitalism, is that the system is running out of options by which to dodge these existential crises. The intensification of globalisation that came from some rather scary moments in the 1970s has not sorted the problem out and nobody can imagine what comes next for capital. Its victims, you and I and the millions of others who see living standards fall and inequality rise and who live with fear and anxiety, appear to have few options, or at least that is how things are portrayed. It has become almost impossible for people to imagine something different. This is the magic of the capitalist system. Over time it has managed to become the dominant paradigm. That is an obvious thing. Being the dominant idea allows it to, well, dominate ideas and thoughts. It was only a couple of generations after the industrial revolution began before the collective memory had adapted to almost believe that capitalism had always been. It ends up a bit like not being able to imagine that which you can't imagine. That shouldn't be the case, but the imagining is dismissed as a fantasy. Socialism, as the obvious counterpoint to capitalism, is the most obvious case. The ways in which one who advocates for socialism can be dismissed are well known. You are naïve, it is just too simplistic, it doesn't and can't work and all the rest. These loaded little platitudes have less currency than they did. The irritating and patronising line that says if you are not a socialist at 20, then you have no heart, and if you are a socialist at 40 then you have no brain, is just that; irritating. However, the fact remains that ideas that actively oppose the mainstream are regarded with hostility by many. This did not happen by accident. It is the product of a long and diligent process of manipulation. Here the state can stand and take a bow.

How it works – the state

The state and capitalism, capitalism and the state. It's not a chicken and egg question. The two are so interconnected and enjoy such a close relationship that it matters not which first drew breath. All that needs to be remembered is that the state has a specific role to play. It exists to facilitate the development of capitalism. It is the state of the ruling idea. Discussions on the state can very quickly become clouded and obscure, so we shall stick to the point. Marxism maintains that the state is ultimately about power and class interests. This does not stop the inevitable analysis. Colin Hay (1999: 153-155), for instance, identifies four separate "Marxist" interpretations of the state – the state as the repressive arm of the bourgeoisie, the state as an instrument of the ruling class, the state as the ideal collective capitalist and the state as a factor of social cohesion. It is not beyond the realms of possibility, or of reason, to suggest that these four interpretations have more than a little in common. The various definitions are, after all, taken from the same sources; those of classical Marxist theorists. If we can accept that the state exists to facilitate capitalism, then it is reasonable to assume that much of the "theoretical" work concerning the state by various interpretations of Marx are simply differing shades of the same colour. The state advantages class interests and depending upon historical and economic conditions can present in any of the above formulations.

Capitalism, over time, assumed a position of dominance. This was achieved with the assistance of a state structure that empowered capitalist relations and overlaid an ideological framework that made meaningful dissent increasingly difficult. Richard Miller describes Marx's conception of the power of ideology within society, stating that "the economically dominant class requires the existence of false beliefs for its dominance and has resources for perpetuating beliefs that are in its interests" (1991: 74). An economic and political structure built on antagonistic class interests cannot expect to survive by force alone. What Marx and Engels labelled "false consciousness" has been a remarkable success. The twentieth century for capitalism was both the best and worst of times. There were moments of crisis that were, in effect, existential moments for capitalism. The century ended, however, with capitalism still largely secure and apparently impervious to challenge. The crises that capitalism experienced failed to result in its demise, not because of any inherent strength of capitalism but in large part because of the role played by the capitalist state itself and the power of an encompassing ideology that saw class conflict minimised. The inherent crisis and the contradictions that capitalism brought with it into the twentieth century, however, remained unresolved as the twenty-first century dawned.

The role of the state in capitalist development has long been a focus for Marxism and for its theory. Chris Harman (1991) offers a useful critique of the relationship between state and capital, or more precisely the role of the state in assisting the development of capitalism. Any pretence that the state and capitalism were in any way separate was once and for all dispelled during the period of the Global Financial Crisis and in its immediate aftermath as the state worked so swiftly, and with such largesse, in response to the potential collapse of significant banks in the US.

Capitalism retains a position of security regardless of the depth of problems and crisis within the economic structure itself. This capacity for capitalism to maintain itself is due, in very large part, to the ideological expertise of the state. Michael Lebowitz (2004) makes the point that capitalism relies on exploitation, but that this became less obvious as the relationship between labour and capital became deliberately obscured. Engels (2000), in his letter to Mehring, offered the view that ideological processes can and often are used to effectively mask what is the real class nature of society. What Marx and Engels described as "false consciousness" was later adapted by Antonio Gramsci to become the idea of cultural hegemony. Under these conditions the ruling class appears to offer concessions in a bargain for both acquiescence and ultimately acceptance of state power. Lebowitz (2004) reflects that if the "left" does not actively seek to both explain capitalism and to advocate for change then it is part of the reason that capitalism survives. This is especially the case when considered against the framework of intensifying capitalist crisis.

This ideological fog has worked well for many decades, but that fog appears to be lifting. Something new seems to be in the air. That very crisis is now affecting every man, woman and child on the planet to varying degrees. To turn on the news is to see cities ablaze. What are described as quite small triggers are moving millions into open revolt. Austerity, corruption, falling and stagnating wages are all acting to catapult people in their millions into struggle. The old formula so long and so well employed by capitalism and its state to ensure acquiescence is losing its power. Worker unrest is rising, there is near to open rebellion in many countries, the right is on the march everywhere. Something has gone terribly wrong.

How does capitalism keep going?

Why then does capitalism survive? How does it cling to life? These are questions that have kept many a theorist wakeful and restless. It is an economic system riven with life-threatening contradictions and if it were a cat then none of its nine lives would remain. What was always difficult for capitalism is becoming critical. It is facing breakdown but is causing many a breakdown at the same time.

We have already talked of the relationship between the state and capital and that the state exists to promote the interests of capitalism. It has magnificently promoted an artificial sense of unity between the classes. Such has been the reality of the past century, but it need not, and nor can it be a projection for the future. The future, after all, is not pre-determined. As Marx so eloquently put it, "Men make their own history, but they do not make it as they please; they do not make it under self-selected circumstances, but under circumstances existing already, given and transmitted from the past" (1986a: 96).

Having said that, it is clear that capitalism survives because people simply can't imagine anything else. Ideas and original thought are shut down as much as is humanly possible. Marx described how the development of capitalism acted to promote such a state of affairs:

> The advance of capitalist production develops a working-class, which by education, tradition, habit, looks upon the conditions of that mode of production as self-evident laws of Nature. The organisation of the capitalist process of production, once fully developed, breaks down all resistance (1986b: 689).

Capitalism maintains its position of ideological power by masking the exploitative nature of the economic system itself. How capitalism works is never explicitly divulged. The idea of the worker "selling" his or her labour power and the extraction of surplus value is a simple enough concept but remains a mystery. The state seeks to ensure that capitalism is not too "visibly" exploitative which leads to a degree of "mystification" of capital itself. We become dependent on capitalism in order to survive, but again the nature of this relationship is never spelled out. And what's more, workers are not simply dependent on capital, but on particular sections of capital. As these sections are often in competition with each other then so too are individual groups of workers in competition with other workers. This serves to intensify an already dependent relationship on capital which, in turn, reduces still further the potential for the development of class consciousness and a desire to change things.

Lebowitz (2004) succinctly describes this reality:

As long as workers have not broken with the idea that capital is necessary, a state under their control will act to facilitate the conditions for the reproduction of capital...Capitalism produces the working class it needs. It produces workers who look upon it as necessary...A system where the reproduction of capital is necessary for the reproduction of wage laborers. What keeps capitalism going? Wage laborers (2004: 24).

Capitalism, at the same time, and in order to keep going, is compelled to expand. This became especially obvious in the 1970s in the face of a crisis that demanded a rapidity in globalisation. Inequality and discontent are connected, and their growth has been linked to the pace of capitalist globalisation. The steady rise in inequality can be observed in individual countries and globally, and with it has come a rise in social discontent. This has manifested itself in both anti-globalisation movements and more recently, in developed economies in both left and, more frequently and alarmingly, right-leaning political and nationalist movements. Globalised capitalist relations have particularly affected the working class as unemployment remains high, industrial and manufacturing production continues to flow from the industrialised states, and welfare state structures have been eroded. Ultimately, this crisis is a consequence of capitalist globalisation, which, in turn, is a by-product of changes that are apparent in world capitalism. The ramifications are obvious.

Figures and statistics concerning the growth of inequality and the concentration of wealth become obsolete as soon as they appear but still, they are worth contemplating. Dallmayr (2002: 144) cites the UN Human Development Report (1999) to show that just three of the wealthiest families in the world enjoy an income equivalent to the poorest 600 million. As I say, statistics change with alarming rapidity as wealth accumulates into fewer and fewer hands. Pieterse (2002: 1025) uses these same figures to indicate a steady and significant growth in inequality since the industrial revolution from a situation in 1820 which saw a gap between the richest fifth of the world's population and the poorest fifth steadily grow from a ratio of 3:1 to 74:1 in 1997. This trajectory has been steadily accelerating and especially since the 1970s. Oxfam figures show that the world's richest 26 individuals control the same wealth as the poorest 3.8 billion people (Oxfam 2019). Credit Suisse (2015) research reveals that nearly three-quarters of the world's population have a per-capita wealth of less than $10,000. Conversely the richest 8 per cent of the population own 84.6 per cent of global wealth. Pieterse asks, "what kind of world economy grows and yet sees poverty and global inequality rising steeply?" (2002: 1036). The answer to his question is not simply a capitalist economy, but one that exists in conditions of irresolvable crisis.

International institutions, analysts and activists alike acknowledge that a fundamentally new stage of crisis has emerged. A report issued by the IMF states that:

> Widening income inequality is the defining challenge of our time. In advanced economies, the gap between the rich and poor is at its highest level in decades. Inequality trends have been more mixed in emerging markets and developing countries (EMDCs), with some countries experiencing declining inequality, but pervasive inequities in access to education, health care, and finance remain (Dabla *et al* 2015: 4).

The OECD (2015) has similarly reported that inequality in OECD countries is at its highest since records began to be kept. The same report indicates that the rise in inequality has been reflected in a growth of part-time and casualised labour. Joint ILO/OECD (2015) research has shown that for decades, labour's share of income has lost ground to capital. OECD (Cingano 2014) reports are also clear that inequality is growing steadily with wealth differentials between rich and poor at their highest in more than 30 years.

As many as 75 per cent of all workers across the globe now fall into the informal category – either as temporary or short-term employees. The growth of capitalist globalisation is mirrored in the growth of the global working class which now sits at about 3.5 billion. One factor that the working class in the OECD world and in the developing world have in common is a growing sense of insecurity.

This sense of insecurity is exemplified in the relationship between capital and labour. In responding to the tendency that exists for a fall in the rate of profits, capital has sought, as it always has, and as it always must do, to maximise the levels of surplus value at its disposal. What appear to be "changes" in the very nature of work are observable as these qualitative changes in capitalism have developed. Traditional labour/capital relationships have been altered. There has been a dramatic rise in the casualisation of labour, "flexible" working arrangements have been introduced, and workers are increasingly regarded as "sub-contractors". Despite these "changes", the reality of that essentially exploitative relationship between capital and labour remains unchanged.

The profound changes in capitalism, and in its quest to maintain profitability, have affected how states operate. This is the case in both developed states and the developing economies. Globalised markets have acted as a motivational force for investors to move capital from the traditionally regulated economic centres to the less regulated. This was initially revealed in accelerated global economic growth but has resulted in increasing instability and insecurity for the working class. What is particularly significant is that the rate of economic growth appears to have stagnated or at least is growing at an unacceptably slow rate (IMF 2016b). While this reflects the underlying problems in capitalism as a crisis-prone system, the fact remains that globalisation was, and is, an attempt to rapidly accelerate economic growth to forestall and circumvent crises stemming from falling profit rates. Its failure to achieve this outcome must keep many a capitalist and many a minister in government awake at night.

Capitalism – haunted and hunted by itself

It's not as though individual or collective capitalists want to dwell in a world that is beset with potentially life-threatening crises. While it is impossible to feel pity for those whose every action drives hundreds of millions into poverty and despair, keeping the wretched machinery of this exploitative machine oiled and ticking over takes some doing.

Capitalism has, from the beginning, been forced to live with its irresolvable contradictions. Admittedly these have at once promoted capitalism's forward motion but could never be resolved. Each step forward simply meant the problems became more deeply entrenched. The essential contradictions have already been described. It must be reiterated that these contradictions initially acted to promote capitalism's growth but, as a response to the expansionary nature of capitalism, its progressive role, as described by Marx in the nineteenth century, is a thing of the past. All that remains is misery.

Marx and Engels wrote of the disorder and crisis that capitalism engenders and of the contradictions that lead to economic crisis. Capitalism and the bourgeoisie, in seeking to manage these critical moments, react and respond by engaging in:

on the one hand enforced destruction of a mass of productive forces; on the other, by the conquest of new markets, and by the more thorough exploitation of the old ones. That is to say, by paving the way for more extensive and more destructive crises, and by diminishing the means whereby crises are prevented (1977: 42).

Its most critical of moments would seem to be the great and possibly final contradiction; a contradiction that can never be resolved, except by the end of capitalism itself. That great and final contradiction is between the objective requirement to globalise and integrate economies and the need to maintain nation-states to administer and facilitate capitalism.

Globalisation, then, leaves capitalism with this final irresolvable contradiction. It is a contradiction of end-of-days proportions, for capital. For capitalism to maintain a sense of stability and continuity it is compelled to expand. At the same time, the nation-state remains the basis for political organisation. While capitalism has by nature always been a globalising force, the economic crisis of the 1970s denoted a dramatic change in these processes, with capitalist relations assuming an increasingly rapid globalising character which has widened and exposed the contradiction between an increasingly borderless economic system and political institutions still limited by geography. Capitalism's quest to maintain profitability in the face of crisis and the ever-present spectre of a falling rate of profit necessarily results in casualties.

The casualties are, as ever, the poor, the working class, the middle class that sits precariously and with fingers crossed that somehow all will stagger back on course. None of this is terribly new. Capitalism has always torn down in order to re-build. Economies and entire states have been destroyed in order to create the world that we have today. At each stage the people have been made to suffer. In good times they are exploited, and their labour enriches capital. In bad times they suffer. Their labour still enriches capital, but the return becomes more painful. Capitalism has always alienated people, but today it has turned alienation into something of an art form. In what were once described as the industrialised countries, we have stagnating wages, insecurity, rising mental health problems, addictions, fear and anxiety about global war and ecological extinction, and the commodification of life itself. In the developing countries there is raw capitalism, ripping and grinding down the people on the altar of profit. Is it any wonder that wherever we turn there is hopelessness and sickness?

Capitalism once operated by the rule of tear down to build up. That is now a thing of history. Its days of building are now in the past. What we are left with is a system in decay and one that is devouring all in its path in its final *danse macabre*. We, the people, whose labour over centuries has provided unimaginable wealth for the few are left, fearfully hoping to survive capitalism's destruction.

Chapter 2

Capitalism, alienation and a cauldron of anxiety

Returning to Roberto and his "sad and beautiful world", we can see just how "sad" it has become. The lab rats are set to scurrying about the maze, but when too much stress is layered onto their lives, they begin to display all sorts of aberrant behaviours. If we look at our world and the people in it, then the stress is palpable, and our maze has become intolerable. We are now all but completely alienated from society, from each other, and from the process of production. We work longer and harder for less return. We are tired. We are compelled to consume the products of capitalism that are out of touch with our needs. We see our children's expectations of life being unfulfilled. We see, on our televisions, a world aflame with anger. We see unimaginable wealth in the hands of fewer and fewer people and we see gross inequalities. Then, as if to rub salt into the wound, we are effectively blamed for the ills of society. Capitalism has all but destroyed the planet and we are burdened with personal and collective guilt. How could we not be alienated?

A lot has been said and a lot has been written about alienation in society. A relatively recent offering is Daniel Burston's *Cyborgs, Zombies and Planetary Death* (2014). He draws our attention to the increasing popularity of the zombie in film and literature. While it is not a terribly subtle analogy, it is nevertheless apt. He states that "at the most basic narrative level, a vampire or zombie is a pseudo-human entity who feeds off our life blood, and therefore seeks to negate human life, or at the very least, to diminish or subdue it in the interests of establishing hegemony for itself and its own kind" (2014: 289). Blunt, unadorned, but at least to the point. Burston, of course, will not be the last to grapple with alienation as it destroys and degrades our world. It is, unfortunately, a rich field for research. For our purpose, it is best to return to the pioneer researcher; Karl Marx. Marx was writing in a particular context and was aiming his critique at a burgeoning capitalism. Marx, in his *Economic and Philosophic Manuscripts of 1844*, outlined this process of alienation that is so inherently a part of capitalist relations:

> What constitutes the alienation of labour? First, the fact that labour is external to the worker, i.e., it does not belong to his essential being...The worker therefore only feels himself outside his work, and in his work feels outside himself... His labour is therefore not voluntary, but coerced; it is forced labour. It is therefore not the satisfaction of a need; it is merely a means for satisfying needs external to it...the external character of labour for the worker appears in the fact that it is not his own but someone else's...it is the loss of self (1984: 110-111).

The working class under such conditions is inevitably estranged, not just by capitalist relations but from capitalist society and from the state itself. The middle class, too, is more and more affected by this deep sense of alienation.

Alienation, for Marx, was an inescapable element of capitalist relations. It was part and parcel of the whole package that capitalism brought to the table. Alienation exists because an antagonistic class-based society exists. He was writing specifically about the working class and its relationship to work and the production process. Work becomes a means to an end and that end is survival, in order to continue the cycle of exploitation. This becomes the unquestioned norm. Marx was quick to point out that we do not naturally come this way. We are social beings and yet are forced to become competitors with others. Workers are pitted against each other and are encouraged to find enemies and rivals where there are none.

But Marx has been dead for an awfully long time

The twenty-first century is well and truly under way. Is there any real point in promoting a view of the world that existed 175 years ago? Things are very different today. Or are they? We live in a world where time appears to have shrunk. Generational changes occur within years rather than decades. There is little by way of collective memory. How can Marx's world equate with our own? These are significant questions and need answering.

Without getting bogged down in Marxist economic and labour theory, it is still necessary to sort out a couple of things that remain important. Marx insisted that when people worked for wages, they were engaging in a transaction. They were selling their labour power. They still do. They produce goods that are turned into money by the employer. Profit as we have seen, derives from "surplus value" and it proceeds from that initial transaction of the "sale" of one's capacity to work, his or her labour power.

This process of selling your capacity to work meant, in Marx's estimation, that labour became just another commodity, that a dehumanising effect could be seen, and that life had no other meaning apart from the process of work. But, of course, this was a long time ago. The dark satanic mills of the industrial revolution are a thing of the past. The developed economies have effectively de-industrialised. What then is to be made of Marx's theory? Surely it is little more than an historical relic, and the stuff of folk songs? That argument might have merit if the production of goods did not still take place. Everything we touch, use, buy, throw away is the result of labour. We might not hear the siren calling alienated workers to the factory bench, but things are still being made by workers. Capitalism expands because it has to. It has no borders, no nationality, no allegiance except to survive and to amass more and more profit; more and more surplus value.

Alright, so we can accept that many of the basic rules of the game that Marx described have not changed. Capitalism is still exploitative, and it has moved much of the most exploitative jobs to developing states. Surely this must equate to a less alienated workforce in the OECD countries? Even if we could excuse the less than casual racism of the argument, an argument that allows for exploitation so long as it is somewhere else, it still needs exploring. Work, whenever there is an unequal relationship, and wherever that might be, is alienating. Whether you are earning third-world or first-world wages is really beside the point. If you are uncertain as to whether you will be getting a wage this time next year, or next month or next week, then you are living with unhealthy stress. If you are fearful of ill-health, of paying the bills, of making sure that your children's education is secure, then you are not enjoying anything like a full and enriching life. You are alienated from others and estranged from the mythologised society that capitalism presents as the good and normal life.

We hear, we read of the worker who is not only content with his or her job, but whose life is defined by that job. Surely these voices, and there are many of them, bring Marx's thesis into question? It is true that not all work is soul-destroying. Many jobs bring satisfaction. There is, at the same time, the undeniable fact that what was once a predictable future has been stolen from even these contented workers. The worker might well say, "I love my job and don't want to retire," but there is that dark cloud of uncertainty that grows as capitalism's crisis grows. The term "precariat" seems to sum things up for these possibly privileged workers rather well. Work is important. It occupies so much of our waking hours and represents so much that becomes stressful for us. It is not the end but the beginning of a journey of alienation.

Work shouldn't make you sick

Thus far, work has been presented as something innately negative. This should not be the case. Work is performed by people and usually in some form of collective arrangement. It is an act that engages people in social interactions, and we are social beings. The problem is that work and production is social and collective while the ownership of that social space remains firmly in private hands. A group of people come together and are immediately separated and divided into individual units of work that are often in competition with one another. Threats hang, unspoken, in the air. We all know how it goes. There will be lay-offs. Will it be me? If I manage to keep my job, then I "win". My co-worker "loses". It is a clash that does not make for happy people. Of course, Marx was talking specifically of the brutal, soul-destroying labour of the industrial age. The point is that nothing significant has changed, except, perhaps, for the worse.

In The Overworked American (1991), sociologist Juliet Schor reported that 30 per cent of Americans experience high stress nearly every day. She makes it clear that Americans are working themselves to death. Schor's study was first published in 1991. By the end of the century, the National Institute for Occupational Safety and Health (1999) revealed survey data showing 80 per cent of American workers felt stress on the job and that 40 per cent experienced "extreme" stress. This, we need to remember, was before the crisis of the GFC in 2008; a crisis from which the world economy is yet to fully recover. Stress as a factor in modern work is growing in all workplaces and in all countries and when we speak of stress, we speak of mental health, physical health, the breakdown of public and private relationships. In short, we see alienation.

There has been an integration of the capitalist economy across the globe and, unsurprisingly, the levels of stress, anxiety and alienation become globalised as well. It hardly matters which nation you use to draw statistics. The picture is much the same across all developed capitalist economies. A recent report produced by Parents at Work (2019) revealed that fully two-thirds of Australian working families struggle to care for their physical and mental health as a result of desperately trying to juggle work and caring for children. A third of families report that this juggling act is placing real strains on relationships. These casualties of capitalist crisis cannot find the time to stay healthy, eat well, exercise and essentially live as they want to and need to.

The nightmare in which we find ourselves begins in the workplace. It matters not whether the labour be physical or intellectual. The end-point is the same. A significant element in all of this is the fragmentation of people and their relationships, and the quite deliberate severing of any form of collective relationship. Where once people were happy to join with others in a range of collective activities – political parties, social organisations, trade unions, clubs – the tendency today is for separation and the inevitable isolation that goes with it. Former British PM Margaret Thatcher in her famous 1987 *Woman's Own* interview gave an honest assessment of how capital regards the people who keep it afloat. She dismissively wrote "society" off when she criticised those who "are casting their problems at society. And, you know, there's no such thing as society. There are individual men and women and there are families. And no government can do anything except through people, and people must look after themselves first."

It was an honest appraisal of where things stood as far as the state and capital were concerned. Thatcher borrowed the idea from the conservative economist Friedrich Hayek. The crisis of capitalism had come to such a point that welfare statism was a luxury that could no longer be afforded. Capitalism and the state had already begun a process that saw the creation of some debased social Darwinism and the survival of the fittest, or the rule of the jungle. Society has been atomised. The debasement begins at work and flows out to every part of our lives. States and capital have not plotted into the night to find ways of making life intolerable. It is an inevitable process that mirrors capitalism's history. It has simply run out of options. It lives with its own nightmare of how to maintain a nation-state system whose task it is to facilitate capitalist development, alongside the necessity of capitalism to continue to integrate unfettered by any consideration of national borders. Capitalism is now best described as "late" capitalism. It has gone about as far as it can go.

An abyss of anxiety

A bleak picture has been painted. Surely things cannot be as bad as that. It would be nice if that were the case but a casual glance at our world, at our neighbourhood, at our own lives and of those around us reveals a terrible truth. We are social creatures now forced to live in social isolation. We have never been more "connected" through social media and yet never have we been more alone. Recent American surveys point to the fact that nearly half of the population almost always feel "alone". More than a third of people in the UK are in the same boat, and 50 per cent of Australians report feeling lonely for at least one day each week.

Society (and despite what Margaret Thatcher might have said, society does exist) is marked by social isolation, addiction, violence, commodification of people, enforced consumerism, narcissism, the love affair with the body and a lunacy that is the media. Taken singly, any of this list can and will end up in unhappiness and despair. The point is that these are not isolated ills of society but the state's collective disease. The causes of that disease are the decaying economic and political structures that corral us, destroy lives and kill too many of us. The growth in suicide rates is just one horrendous statistic that damns capitalism. OECD (2019) figures reveal that for each 100,000 of population, 10.2 Germans, 11.8 Canadians, 11.9 Australians and 13.9 Americans die by suicide each year. The figures appear to get worse as the difficulties of living in an impossible world increase.

Is it any wonder then that nobody seems to be getting a decent night's sleep? Johann Hari sprang to prominence with the book *Chasing the Scream* (2016). It presents a strong case for drug reform. The catch-phrase that the book introduced is that the opposite of addiction is not sobriety but human connection. The rights or wrongs of the war on drugs, or whether they should be decriminalised, or not, is not the point and has little direct impact on this discussion. Hari's comment is important for our discussion as it cuts to the chase when considering the dehumanisation that accompanies late capitalism. The troubles of the age are such that individuals and groups inevitably focus on this or that problem as "the" problem. Addiction, for example, has become such a problem that its victims are counted in the tens and hundreds of millions across the world. In the US, as just one example, there are 21 million people with at least one addiction. From the economic point of view, it is a crisis that costs the US economy $600 billion annually. It hardly matters which country you wish to look at, the crisis is all but universal. The addiction may be alcohol, or drug-related, or gambling, or electronic-device driven. It does not require much imagination to link these crises and it is hardly surprising to hear that in the US as an example, fully 20 per cent of all people suffering from depression also live with an addiction.

The aberrant behaviour of the rats in capitalism's maze all too often end in harm. This may be either to the self or to others. Violence, be it domestic, sexual or physical, or violence perpetrated by stranger upon stranger, are yet more signs of decay and debasement. None of these behaviours can be excused but so many can be explained. Stress, alienation, powerlessness, all play a part in turning our societies into such dangerous places. What prompts someone to open fire on a crowded street? The media, anxious for a salacious headline, will decry the "evil" of the murderer but far less frequently will the reporter ask about how a society can become so dysfunctional, so diseased, as to allow for the gathering and reporting of statistics such as how many crimes of domestic violence are committed annually, or how many deaths are the result of prescription drugs, or how many mass shootings there have been, and then to blithely move on. The statistics are given, and the public pay less and less attention. They can't. It is not as if they do not feel the collective pain, but life gets in the way. Surviving the system becomes the priority. The state and its servants in the media redouble their efforts to keep the people from the unpalatable truth. A piece of wall graffiti once captured the mood: 6consume, be silent, die!

When consuming becomes an almost patriotic duty

Capitalism survives because workers create products that are sold to consumers. These consumers are, not at all surprisingly, workers. A beautiful sleight of hand is enacted. The worker sells his or her labour power, receives a portion of its value as a wage and then is compelled to give it back in exchange for goods, some of which sustain life but increasingly goods that are deemed by capital to "enhance" life. Capitalism stays afloat first by the labour of the worker and then by the consumption of the worker. This is hardly an act of largesse on the part of the capitalist but more appropriately a double dose of exploitation. There is a blanket bombing by the media to make sure that we do the "right" thing and become both worker and valiant consumer. Globally, advertising is now worth more than $1.2 trillion. A trillion dollars a year to convince us to buy products we don't really want, far less need. You have to admit it. It is really a very clever system.

If consumption stopped, then capitalism and the global

economy would come crashing down. As it is, when consumption slows the economic system becomes very nervous. The Federal Reserve Bank of St Louis (one of 12 regional reserve banks that make up the US Central Bank) has some rather interesting things to say about the power of the consumer (FRED 2103). In 1929, just before the great stock market crash, consumer spending accounted for 75 per cent of the US economy. WWII saw this figure significantly fall, with a subsequent rise in the 1950s and 60s to about 62 per cent. Today it sits at 71 per cent. Comparable figures for other advanced capitalist economies are similarly weighted. Consumption, however, can hardly be expected nor allowed to stop. There is too much at stake. To suggest that it might spell the end of capitalism is certainly one way of looking at the problem, but the opinion-moulders can spin things a little differently. If consumption stops or slows appreciably, then production slows and workers will lose their jobs. So, it ends up being our fault. Why should we be surprised? We are exhorted almost daily to spend, spend, spend. After all the future of the world, as we know it, depends on us. We keep the economy going. It is our duty to consume. We have grown accustomed to this. Consumption, regardless of need, has been normalised, but then the state has a long and successful history of convincing the people that what is good for capitalism is, necessarily, good for us all. The success of capitalism's salesmanship in this regard was highlighted by Arthur Burns in *The Business Cycle in a Changing World*. He enthusiastically wrote that "consumer spending has played a more dynamic role in recent times. Not only have consumers managed their spending during recessions so that the cumulative process of deflation has been curbed, but consumer spending has emerged as one of the active factors in arresting recession and hastening recovery" (1969: 115).

We have received the message loud and clear. "Good" citizens buy the products of capitalism. It is, however, hard to be good when the same capitalist market doesn't provide the wherewithal to allow us the discretionary income to be the "best" consumer possible. The OECD Report *Under Pressure: The Squeezed Middle Class* (2019a) points to a galloping growth in inequality. Broken down by decade, income growth for "middle-income" households across the OECD was 1.0 per cent from the 1980s-1990s; 1.6 per cent from the mid-1990s to the mid-2000s; and just 0.3 per cent from 2007-2016. What it all means is that people across the world are engaged in a daily struggle to survive. The days of continued real-wage growth are a fading memory. The OECD report was focusing purely on the middle class. Is it realistic to assume that the working class are faring any better? Any way that you care to look at it, there is a problem.

Consumption makes the world go round. It is good for society. This is the myth that our image-makers peddle. They don't go quite as far or have quite the cheek to use the slogan Aldous Huxley invented for his *Brave New World* – "ending is better than mending" – but they might as well. It's the way we live now. This is not said in the cause of any nostalgic dewy-eyed vision of the past. It is not said with the idea of promoting an austere world of want. Writing as a Marxist, the future can be seen as one with planned plenty, which stands in contrast to the anarchy of gorging that capitalism demands. The nightmarish world of Huxley's imagination survived because its economy was based on consumption and ever more consumption. Obviously, such a world has limits. The elastic can only stretch so far, as we are seeing with capitalism in the twenty-first century.

The truth that capitalism is in such deep crisis is something that needs to be kept, as much as possible, from the public gaze. To make anything like a public admission that things are out of control would only make us even more insecure, fearful and anxious than we already are. Engendering panic is never the best policy option. Government spokespeople, ministers and the like reassure us that things are really going along swimmingly.

There might be some "headwinds" or whatever the latest fashionable code word might be for an incoming hurricane, but the "fundamentals are sound". If that doesn't resonate well enough, then we are urged, cajoled, to spend more, to promote growth. After all we don't want to be responsible for a collapse of the economy. We don't want to be the cause of job losses. Far too many continue to heed the call, despite being unable to afford such dubious "patriotism". The stock in trade of the state apparatus for centuries now has been to inculcate a feeling of unity. We are all in this together. We are all Americans or British or Australians. Our nationality comes before any other consideration. If there are problems, then it is probably the fault of some nameless or, worse, some named outside influence and so the record plays and replays.

People are not stupid. They can see through this, but they are also tired, stressed, cling to a fading hope that someone, somewhere knows what is going on and is doing something. Someone has to be in charge. While the walls crumble about us, diversions and distractions become the order of the day. Can people really be blamed for turning away from reality and allowing the fantasy of capitalism to wash over them?

What then is real?

As life in late capitalism becomes ever more dislocated, disjointed and dysfunctional, so too are people presented with ever more stupefying attractions and distractions. Huxley's people of *Brave New World* had the universal drug soma, electronic games that ensured a "feel-good" outcome and the "feelies" that enabled the public to experience the unreality that they saw on the screen. The poor benighted citizens of Ray Bradbury's *Farenheit 451* could escape reality and were encouraged in the escape by the interactive "wall" screens. This is, of course, fiction. We are so fortunate that nothing like that has invaded our world or our minds.

Mass pursuits that exist to turn our attention from reality are nothing new. They existed before capitalism and were seized upon by the new economic and political reality to keep people on-side. Mass entertainments, radio, cinema, television and the delights of the electronic age are all simply refinements. Surely there can be nothing sinister in this. The people deserve recreation and to have things that are different, that divert them from the humdrum of existence. This is undoubtedly true, but we continue to see some rather disturbing signs. In 1997, Bob Franklin in *Newszak and News Media* observed that:

> entertainment has superseded the provision of information; human interest has supplanted the public interest; measured judgement has succumbed to sensationalism; the trivial has triumphed over the weighty; the intimate relationships of celebrities, from soap operas, the world of sport or the royal family are judged more "newsworthy" than the reporting of significant issues and events of international consequence. Traditional news values have been undermined by new values; "infotainment" is rampant (1997: 4).

Can we, with anything like a straight face, say that things have improved in the past 2 decades since those lines were written? Apparently, we can take heart. At least one academic is prepared to stand firm and defend what has become of the media. Mick Temple (2006) is steadfast in arguing that the "dumbing down" of political and news coverage is simply a process that engages people in debates. According to this line of thinking, "the public has choice...they are capable of constructing their own individualized public sphere. Politics, like any largely mediated activity, must seek an audience but it may also need to create an audience. That audience will be one whose engagement with politics has been primarily mediated through popular entertainment such as talk shows or reality programmes" (2006:

271-272). These sorts of arguments can only serve to confuse. Temple's article is entitled *Dumbing Down is Good for You*. Nobody will be surprised if you don't accept the argument.

There is little to be gained in plunging into a protracted debate about the idea of postmodernism, but it does fit beautifully with a worldview that sees the individual as the centre of things and ideas as being simply reflections of an individualist set of perceptions. Any idea is as good as any other. History is what you want it to be. That sort of thing. The problem is that it is but one more expression of a society that is atomised. The media is an enormously powerful weapon in the armoury of the state. It has acted to isolate us. We become prey to whatever idea is put into our head. The person who speaks last wins the argument. Now this is a sweeping generalisation. Millions of people struggle against such a devastating world, but the collective voice becomes muted in the morass of individualism.

What is even more disturbing when considered in relation to the deep alienation that capitalism has and is engendering in people is a correlation between "entertainments" and mental health issues. In the last 2 decades there has been an explosion in the genre of "reality" television. They are produced at a fraction of the cost of "traditional" television. If you cast your mind back you will remember entertainments with actors, writers, directors and the rest, producing material for the free-to-air market. Those that survive are increasingly vanishing from the "traditional" platforms. They have been replaced by "reality" shows that see the performers undergoing a range of ritual humiliations but generally without union-negotiated fees for performance. It all fits with the image of the individual cast adrift on a sea of anxiety. In 2019, reports surfaced of the numbers of participants on these shows who have suicided after the ritual humiliation that capital demanded of them. Numbers of deaths from among these "stars" vary from the low 20s to high 30s in the past decade. It is an indictment of the vicious nature of an economic system that places no value on human life.

Capitalism and its media are growing more and more irresponsible. The same reality television shows that are killing the participants are having devastating effects on audiences as well. Britain's Mental Health Foundation (2019) has revealed statistics that reality television shows have led 24 per cent of 18-24-year-olds to "worry" about body image. The same report shows that advertising and promotions via social media have resulted in 23 per cent of young Britons having had suicidal thoughts concerning body image.

Each wave, each development in mass communication has had the potential to liberate. Each development has, in so many ways, been used to enslave. It is a paradox that mirrors the entire development of capitalism and of its inevitable exploitation, estrangement and alienation. Capitalism was once a progressive force for change. It drove innovation, pushed thinking and allowed for flights of fancy. It also marshalled ideas to suit its interests. Among these were mass communications, the development of the newspaper being a major case in point. It allowed the new ruling class to promote its ideology but also offered opportunities to spread other ideas. Obviously, the state's conception of a "free press" might be different from those who wish to change the status quo. It has been the case ever since. The advent of the internet offered capital a mighty opportunity and simultaneously allowed for communications between people in an unprecedented way. Fast forward a few decades and we see negatives. For many, the liberator becomes the oppressor. In the words of James Reveley, with a:

semblance of active participation in social media, the possibility of uploading materials or commenting on existing ones, of sharing Facebook "likes" with others, no doubt perpetuates the...myth of consumer sovereignty. Social media users choose to do these things. It is this conscious participation in a process that ultimately results in commodification of personal information stripped from the user, and its reconfiguration for targeted advertising (2013: 86-87).

The use of the word "choosing" here is exceedingly important. What degree of choice is there when an entire apparatus of state, capital and its institutions all decree that we become consumers, that we become commodities, that information, private and public, has a dollar value added?

When ideas go wrong

Personal information becomes commodified, as must everything within the world of capitalism. To turn our thoughts, ideas and individuality into potential markets is to show an alienated world and a world in deep crisis. How to combat this, from an increasingly individualised, atomised society, becomes difficult. "Dumbing down", we have been told, is "good for us". To rail against the media, or its master, is nothing especially new. George Orwell famously described a situation in 1984, whereby the language is deliberately reduced. Doubtless the rulers would argue that this made communications simple and convenient, but significantly it all but precluded any capacity for dissent. Things were either good or un-good, plus or double plus good or un-good. Orwell was, of course, writing at the time when the cold war was getting started, and authoritarianism was a legitimate target. For Orwell, however, it was not just the Soviet Union that was at fault. In his essay, *Politics and the English Language* (1968), he argued forcefully that the language of our political masters had a special role of making lies appear to be truth. While there have been many critics of the way language has been used, conscripted and debased for political purposes, the media, in recent decades, has shifted gear and focus. Language shrinks, but the entire notion of mass entertainment has begun to take on a more grotesque shape. The commodified person, the individual in a world that is simply too big to contemplate, has only the self to rely on. It is not enough.

One of the problems that we face when looking at what is wrong and how to go about fixing things is that there are so many things that are broken. Let us say, for the sake of convenience, that we could isolate 20 separate problems. It would be a simple enough job to find 20 separate "menders" out there. Each would focus on one problem, as *the* problem. The point remains that the problems all have one root cause. That cause is capitalism and its inability to offer anything except insecurity, inequality, fear and anxiety. Capitalism, though, is rarely identified as the culprit. Research and scholarship would seem to demand that individuals focus on individual ills, even if that serves to reinforce the problem. Some researchers do come close. Matthew McDonald, Stephen Wearing and Jess Ponting, for example, present an account for the rise in narcissism. They regard neo-liberalism as the cause. "As an ideology we contend that neo-liberal economic, social and political relations, has led to a distinct form of alienation that we conceptualize as narcissism. Narcissism offers an interpretation of alienation from the defining characteristics of neo-liberal free market societies – individualism and consumerism" (2013: 489-490). Narcissism is identified as a problem but is described as a by-product of an attempt at constructing self-identity, which in turn becomes commodified.

This linkage between the atomisation of society, the commodification of the self and the decay of capitalism revolves, in the thinking of many, around the idea of self-identity. It is an idea that is well worth considering. Identity has become a dominant theme in political life in the past few decades. Identity politics has been prominently described as a quest to belong. Manuel Castells, in promoting this perspective, has remarked that "identity is people's source of meaning and experience" (2004: 6). To seek identity, to belong, in the face of an intensely alienating society is understandable and especially so as capitalist globalisation is rightly presented as destructive of identity and autonomy. Once upon a time, before Thatcher's denial of society arguments, before capitalism simply ran out of ideas, in a time when we could, with a bit of luck, still get a decent night's sleep, our identity was marked by our relative position in society. Class was the determining factor of identity. An artificial splintering has occurred. Class has been relegated in favour of the politics of identity.

Chapter 3

The alienated politics of identity

If alienation and anxiety are direct results of an economic and political system that is in deep crisis, then it is only logical to assume that there would be voices raised against this very system. It is a reasonable assumption and, yes, there are those voices and yes, they are raised frequently and often loudly. What has happened, over the past few decades, is that the politics of anti-capitalism have undergone a most interesting transformation. They have moved from the politics of class to the politics of identity. Now this might seem a bit like hair splitting but a social class is, by definition, a rather big thing. Your identity, on the other hand, possibly based on race, ethnicity, gender or sexuality, might be relatively small by comparison.

Before we get too deeply involved with this discussion, it would be well to remember that ever since the rise of capitalism, there has been a political and ideological war, sometimes waged in the open and sometimes below the surface. On one side sits the state and capitalism. On the other is Marxism and the idea of a socialist alternative. While there are ranges of opinions that smudge or colour this interpretation, there are essentially just two ideas.

Marxism stood and still stands as the anthesis of capitalist rule. The past century has been a difficult one for Marxism. It has existed in a disputed terrain and has been besmirched by Stalinism. Unfortunately, there are still many who equate Stalinism with Marxism. Some go so far as to draw a political genealogy connecting Stalin to Marx. However, the point is that Marxism remains as capitalism's implacable ideological foe. Marxism historically placed particular emphasis on the centrality of the working class as a means of effecting economic, political and societal change. A century of discord has led to this emphasis becoming increasingly muted. There is an interesting link, seldom acknowledged, between the rise in alienation in late capitalism and the fragmentation of elements within the Marxist heritage. It is well worth considering, especially from the perspective of the growth in significance of identity politics. This burgeoning of identity politics highlights the ideological dilemma faced by Marxism since the 1960s and the development of New Left politics. It also holds a mirror to the atomisation of society in late twentieth and early twenty-first century capitalist society.

We live in a world where the collective memory has become rather short. The politics of identity is a relatively recent arrival. How and why it appeared is important. What were the motivations behind its original ideologists? How did it manage to capture the hearts and minds of so many? How did it become an almost "mainstream" form of political expression? What are the weaknesses that are so inherent in this approach to combatting capitalism? Answering these questions allows us to ask and respond to others. Why does the state, the same state that exists to facilitate capitalist development, permit and, if obliquely, promote the politics of identity? How is identity politics a symbol of the alienation that is consuming so many?

Identity politics versus the politics of class

It's not that difficult to accept that capitalism is the problem, that it offers nothing but inequality, despair and alienation. We know that it is riven by crisis. It's not all that hard to accept that Marxism, that socialism has the answer, but still capitalism remains. What then is going on? Let's start with Marx and return to a few simple and, I hope, acceptable truths. Capitalism's survival is predicated on the appropriation of surplus value. Capitalist society is built on an economic base, upon which rests a political and social superstructure. The state, as facilitator of the dominant economic ideology, is rooted in class and class divisions. These are issues that define Marxism. Ultimately there is one capitalism. Sure, it adapts, while always seeking, but never successfully, to escape its inherent contradictions. There can, at the end of the day, be only one Marxism capable of issuing a successful challenge to capitalist rule.

There have been many departures from the essence of Marxist theory, but the most telling has been the move away from class as the pivotal issue, which is odd given that there is a continually expanding working class that is constantly being created by capitalism. By 2030 there will be 3.5 billion members of the global working class (Dobbs *et al* 2012).

And, while the working class grows, the merits of identity politics have been promoted ahead of class politics, despite the existence of this working class that logically, potentially and realistically could be drawn into the struggle against capitalism. The working class exists, its aspirations are antagonistic to those of capitalism, and it is constantly under threat as the crisis of capitalism deepens. To not place class at the centre of things simply defies logic. A question hangs in the air: what forces exist that can take on the system and change the world? There would seem to be a rather simple answer to that question.

Does the working class, then, have "revolutionary potential?" Regardless of poor leadership, or periods of apparent indifference, it does remain a potentially revolutionary force. Three things show this:

1. The working class is the class that, by its labour, produces and reproduces capitalist production;
2. The needs of opposing classes remain intensely contradictory; and
3. The working class has become an increasingly globalised class as capitalism itself has become a globalised economic structure.

But there remains an odd reluctance to acknowledge the potential power of the working class. Theorists often dance around the edges. There are many instances. Two deserve sharing. Ricardo Fuentes-Ramirez (2014) vigorously argues that change can be won by influencing the state to empower institutions that might, in turn, cause "ruptures" within capitalist institutions. It is a fantastical idea. To separate state institutions from capitalist institutions and then use one against another would seem a bit unlikely. David Harvey (2012: 157) can see "glimmers" of hope. We all like glimmers. His are, or were, based on the left-populist movements in Spain and Greece and on what he describes as "revolutionary impulses" in Latin America. History can move quickly and often does. Harvey's "glimmers" are now very faint. He was, when writing that analysis, strongly influenced by the *Occupy Wall Street Movement*, but Occupy came and went, leaving barely a trace. He proposes that the anti-capitalist movement should connect with the alienated and discontented and that this "movement" might provide an alternative way of organising production, distribution and consumption for the benefit of the people. Nice, but how is this change to be brought about and which forces will bring about change? Class, no matter how it might be downplayed, is never far away.

Class identification can be a subjective thing, but a Marxist understanding of class is not. At its simplest, class can be determined by where one lines up in relation to the ownership of the means of production, distribution and exchange. "It is always the direct relationship of the owners of the conditions of production to the direct producers" (Marx 1986: 791). It is a world of division. Such divisions cannot help but be antagonistic. They lead to social inequality and, ultimately, to class awareness.

Despite all this, identity theorists still hold the line. Some go so far as to claim that it is the only "valid" response to inequality. Manuel Castells cheerfully informs us that the "ideological emptiness created by the failure of Marxism-Leninism was replaced, in the 1980s, when people were able to express themselves, by the only source of identity in the collective memory: *national identity*" (2004: 43). If Castells is correct, then the sources of inequality ought to have been identified, organised against, challenged and, by sheer dint of the "superiority" of the theory, inequality ought to be declining rather than rising so sharply. The palpable sense of fear, anxiety, alienation that is being felt across the world ought to be diminishing, but it is rising. Something seems to be wrong with the theory.

To deny class is to ignore the magnitude of the billions-strong global working class and, in large measure, to ignore Marxism. The two are, after all, inseparable. To weaken one, weakens the other. Capitalism's ability to "keep going", or to reproduce itself, is due in large part to the acquiescence of the working class – something that the state has worked so well in maintaining.

This is all very well. Even a cursory look at things shows it to be true. Unfortunately, facts don't always count, when political careers and the careers of political theorists are being built. The fact of the matter is that in the eyes of much of what constitutes the "left", class is not what it is all about. Many go so far as to virtually deny the existence of the working class altogether.

Goran Therborn (2012) describes what he sees as the passing of the "working class century" and argues that a new era with new relationships that mix class, nation and ideology will become the focus of challenge to capitalism. Therborn speaks of the twentieth century as the century of the working class while the twenty-first century represents a shift to the middle class. It is an idea that is broadly accepted by many theorists and by many who claim the title of Marxist. Therborn does accept that capitalist exploitation and oppression continue and asks who will put their stamp upon the new century and the struggles against capitalism – the "new" middle class or those he so dismissively describes as the "plebeian" masses. Having declared the century of the working class to be over, he ultimately offers a defeatist and demoralised perspective.

Ernesto Laclau and Chantal Mouffe are quite definitive in their conceptions of the future of Marxist thought:

> Only if we renounce any epistemological prerogative based upon the ontological privileged position of a "universal class", will it be possible to discuss the present day degree of validity of the Marxist categories...It is no longer possible to maintain the conception of subjectivity and classes elaborated by Marxism, nor its vision of the historical course of capitalist development (2001: 2-4).

If we can get past the nearly impenetrable language, the meaning still rings out clearly. Their claim is that class analysis is next to useless and a new, better way of thinking is required. By definition that new thinking is "their" thinking. It is easy to slip into dogmatic positions. These theorists are entitled to think and write whatever they wish. The point is that, ultimately, ideas are proven or disproven by what happens on the ground. History moves swiftly at times and ideas that are found wanting can sometimes litter the historical landscape. If it were possible to accept this negative view of things, then we would be left with the idea that class does not cut it anymore and, logically, the politics of identity as a new and "better" idea should be able to challenge the power of capitalism. This is not to say that identity is unimportant. It is important. It gives self-worth and more so when society is increasingly atomised. However, whether the left is building opposition or playing a part in the alienation process is quite another question.

The mysterious rise of identity politics
Identity politics began its ascendency in the period immediately before capitalism entered a new and intensely deep crisis. The

immediate post-WWII period was a good time for capitalism. The war was over, rebuilding capitalist economies was the order of the day, and the politics of Stalinism ensured that there would be little by way of fight-back by the working class. Buoyant economies allowed for seemingly harmonious relationships between employer and worker. The result, during this brief "golden age", was an acquiescent working class, a relatively affluent society and a growth in liberal attitudes. It was the age of radical youth culture, the entry of working-class youth into universities, anti-colonial and national liberation movements and a questioning of the old verities. It was also a period that began to place the individual over the collective. People were still aware of injustice and sought ways and means of promoting causes that would fight for a just world. It was just that class was declared to be no longer the answer. Enter the politics of identity.

There were many theorists who promoted identity as a political pathway. Manuel Castells serves as a symbol of the thinking that developed and promoted the idea. He forcefully argues that identity assumes a political character and is portrayed as a means of rallying like-minded individuals, as well as presenting a means of combatting the "institutions" of society that form the basis of oppression (2004: 8). He also maintains (2000) that working-class decline can be partially attributed to the rise of identity politics in the 1960s and 1970s and that the working class can no longer be regarded as the primary actor that will precipitate change.

Identity politics appeared to offer itself as a suitable vehicle in seeking to construct a political framework that might confront broadly defined institutions of "oppression". Identity politics, it was claimed, expressed "the principle that identity – be it individual or collective – should be central to both the vision and practice of radical politics...Identity politics also expresses the belief that identity itself – its elaboration, expression, or affirmation – is and should be a fundamental focus of political work" (Kauffman 2001: 23). And so, it came to pass.

The 1970s (as the crisis in capitalism reached a new and fundamentally critical moment) saw a dramatic rise in political movements that focused on identity issues. Frances Fox Piven (1995) argues that the expansion of capitalism and its globalising character has acted to weaken and destroy the more traditional working-class politics of resistance. She contends that globalisation was the catalyst for the rise of racial, ethnic, religious and gender conflicts and that identity politics is its inevitable consequence. Piven makes two contradictory claims. Identity politics at once "makes people susceptible to the appeals of modern nationalism, to the bloody idea of loyalty to state and flag, which is surely one of the more murderous ideas to beset humankind" (1995: 105). She simultaneously describes the politics of identity as "a potentially liberating and even equalizing development, especially among subordinate groups, and the more so in a political culture already dominated by identity politics" (Piven 1995: 106). In other words, identity politics is useful when identity politics already exists.

What is particularly relevant in all of this is how pervasive the idea of identity politics has become. It would seem almost anathema for Marxists, whose purpose has always been to advocate a class perspective and therefore to confront capitalism through class struggle, to adopt and adapt to a philosophy that is really so different. But that is what has happened. Little by little, almost unconsciously the changes came about. The development of identity politics was at first criticised among Marxists whose engagement was in the area of political activism. Sharon Smith (1994) argues that identity politics fails to offer a realistic framework for those wishing to transform society. There is a degree of irony in this. Activist politics that come from Marxist, socialist or communist roots have almost exclusively developed a conscious focus on the politics of identity, despite having initially decried the ideology. The programmes and policy statements of almost all political parties with a Marxist orientation, regardless of whether they trace their heritage to Stalinist or non-Stalinist perspectives, declare that they stand for the replacement of capitalism. At the same time, these parties strongly advocate for political activism that is, in essence, non-class in nature but an activism that supports individual and group rights. While not seeking to diminish such advocacy, the question as to how capitalism is challenged by waging campaigns around what are essentially non-class issues, remains unanswered.

The weakness of the idea

Non-class political movements, in the form of identity politics, have built strong constituencies. This is an obvious fact. They have achieved concessions from state institutions, while not eroding state power or capitalism. Herein lies the rub. If capitalism is the problem, then capitalism ought to be the primary target. Whatever the focus of a campaign defined by identity, it simply does not and nor can it challenge the basic premise of capitalism. This is not to suggest that the issues that identity politics clothes itself in are not important. They all identify issues that are symptomatic of the ills of capitalist society. They are all issues that mark out a society that privileges one group over another but are all issues that might as easily be regarded as human rights issues that can be resolved without the economic and political system being challenged in the slightest. Social inequality, economic inequality, the commodification of everything and everyone, the exploitation of people in the entire economic structure that is capitalism are, as we have already seen, making us mad. The basis of identity politics is to overcome one problem, when all problems are linked. The sense of being isolated and alone within the borders of your "identity" group can only end in further alienation. Josie Appleton (2019) speaks of the erosion of mediation between individuals and the broader society and of how this leads to an increased level of estrangement. She argues that identity politics can be regarded as distancing the individual from the social.

A consequence of the shift to identity politics has been the realisation that identity, as a political focus, can and does limit the potential to present any real challenge to the underlying conditions. It is intensely difficult for activists to conform to the boundaries that identity politics appear to erect. Struggles are often arranged around issues of colour, of ethnicity, of religion, of sexuality. Some of these have an immediate sense of connectivity. Others do not. There are times when the separation and then integration of differing issues verges on the absurd. Gabriel Ignatow, for instance, describes the work of the African-American Environmentalist Association, whose goals are "to increase African-American participation in the environmental movement, promote an African-American point of view in American environmental policy..." (2007: 1). The way some single-issue, identity movements are inescapably interconnected with other movements has led to moves to link movements and to discover what unites movements.

This realisation gave birth to the concept of *intersectionality* in radical political movements. The concept of intersectionality is often attributed to Kimberle Crenshaw. She argues that "the problem with identity politics is not that it fails to transcend differences...but rather the opposite – that it frequently conflates or ignores intragroup differences" (1991: 1242). She uses the issues of race and gender as a case in point and seeks to broaden the argument to become potentially more inclusive of differences in primary focus. While this theory does take account of the limiting nature of identity politics it remains locked into a non-class approach to understanding inequality. However, regardless of the web of interwoven identities, a problem remains. Marx described the advent of a distribution of labour and the class nature of society, whereby each person "has a particular, exclusive sphere of activity, which is forced upon him and from which he cannot escape" (1964: 44). Marx wrote of the limiting nature of workers being identified by trade or the "type" of work undertaken. Identification within a much greater group offers a greater capacity to effect change. In this case class identification becomes immensely stronger than that of individual trades. A narrow political alignment based on personal identification, like a designated role in the production process, limits the potential for change and emancipation. The idea of intersectionality certainly goes some way toward recognising this fact. At the same time, it is still a limited response to what are broader issues of exploitation that stem, ultimately, from capitalism itself.

Feminist politics, and particularly the debates around patriarchy, have fuelled the growth in identity politics. Carole Pateman (1988) argues that patriarchy long pre-dates capitalist oppression, and that the relationship of sexual domination is a separate oppressive structure to that of capitalism. She rejects the notion that individuals "freely" engage in property exchange or, more significantly, in the sale of labour power. This is true to an extent, or at least in a literal reading of the issue. There is more coercion than freedom employed. Pateman's view is that such a conception is a "fiction" that masks patriarchal domination. A more satisfactory argument is that with the division of labour, and with the emergence of class-based societies, patriarchal organisation dominated. Capitalism, as it developed, simply used that which was already the norm. Conscious attempts were made to unify Marxist analyses of patriarchy with feminist critiques, but the results have not been a resounding success. Patriarchy is deeply rooted in society and it is older than capitalism. Whether it is "more fundamentally oppressive than capitalism", as some maintain, is a debatable issue. It is capitalism that remains the central issue and problem. Capitalism's use of ideology to promote illusions that patriarchy, or race, or ethnicity, are separate issues and detached from capital itself allow it to maintain divisions among people.

Political responses to capitalism, globalisation and the alienation that this generates are inescapable. The position of the working class as a force for fundamental change has been relegated, in the thinking of many, to a position of relative insignificance. Broad, non-class and supra-class movements have mobilised huge numbers of people and have united diverse sections of the population. For many, social movement politics offers a vehicle to successfully confront capitalism. For others, the very supra-class nature and limitations of programme, inherent in such movements, become clearly defined.

The state and the politics of identity

There would appear to be a paradox. The politics of identity has, ostensibly, been developed as a means to fight against inequality, injustice and the wrongs of a society that is making life more and more difficult. That sounds reasonable. After all, ever since there has been exploitation, there has been resistance. The paradox lies in the fact that the state, whose task it is to maintain order, and facilitate capitalist development, appears content to allow for the politics of dissent to comfortably exist alongside the politics of appropriation and exploitation.

Manuel Castells (2004: 7-8), in addressing the theory of identity politics, outlines three connected issues that are associated with "identity". These are "legitimising", "resistance" and "project" identity. It is in the area of resistance identity that the theory assumes special significance and all the more so in light of this paradox. Resistance identity, Castells explains, is generated "by those actors who are in positions/conditions devalued/ stigmatized by the logic of domination, thus building trenches of resistance and survival on the basis of principles different from, or opposed to, those permeating the institutions of society" (Castells 2004: 8). In other words, identity is seen to assume a political character and is portrayed as a means of rallying like-minded individuals, as well as presenting a means of combatting the "institutions" of society that form the basis of oppression. Castells also argues (2000) that working-class decline can be partially attributed to the rise of identity politics in the 1960s and 1970s and that the working class can no longer be regarded as the primary actor that will precipitate change. There is a certain logic that may be ascribed to such a proposition, but it is a most unsatisfactory logic.

LA Kauffman describes the process of identity politics as expressing "the principle that identity – be it individual or collective – should be central to both the vision and practice of radical politics...Identity politics also expresses the belief that identity itself – its elaboration, expression, or affirmation – is and should be a fundamental focus of political work" (2001: 23). Now we are not engaging in a polemic, but it is of passing interest to consider the power of language. Kauffman's arguments certainly have a ring of authenticity about them but there is that nagging question – what is this "political work"? If it is simply to campaign against a social injustice or inequity, then yes, identity politics might be the best vehicle, but if anybody is trying to focus on the bigger picture, of trying to come to terms with just what is happening and why capitalism continues to tear us apart, then these "politics", while interesting, can be of no real significance. If they were, then would the same state that exists to support capitalism tolerate such actions?

This is not intended to sound mean-spirited. Those engaging in any range of identity politics campaigns are doing so from the best and noblest of motives. They want change but the only option being presented is arguably leading them into a cul-de-sac of confusion. There will be victories. Rights, that are often best described as human rights, will be won, but capitalism will not have lost an inch of ground. Just struggles around all, or any, of the issues of the day can be waged by those espousing an anti-capitalist programme, or equally by conservative politicians. We might remember that marriage equality was won in Australia after the conservative government introduced legislation for it. Tony Blair introduced Britain's Human Rights Act, and the Civil Rights Act of 1964 in the US became law under Lyndon Johnson. Change was brought about and has been brought about so many times, but capitalism and its state remain comfortably in place. American academic James R Rogers (2019) portrayed the outcome of much of identity politics that promote anti-capitalist or socialist ideas as actually preventing the advancement or achievement of fundamental socialist aims rather than advancing them.

Rogers' arguments are closely linked to some of the more enduring debates and polemics that have raged with the Marxist movement for the better part of a century. The debates were around just what was to be done, how objectives were to be achieved, and whether it was possible to reform capitalism into something resembling socialism or whether a more fundamental, revolutionary road was to be taken. It is probably an understatement, but the reforming path has been the path of choice for most anti-capitalist movements and especially those adhering to identity politics. It is not much of an understatement to say that the success rate of such a path has been abysmal. After a century of reformist politics and 4 decades of persistent identity politics campaigns, capitalism remains unchallenged.

It is sometimes necessary to be blunt. If such political activism were to be successful and if it were to be outrageously successful, then capitalism would, at the very best, become more tolerable. There is a problem with this. While the activists are fighting to make capitalism less horrendous in the here and now, the system continues to degenerate and, by necessity, becomes more exploitative and alienating. It cannot be any other way. The sad irony is that the more successful the identity campaign is now, the worse becomes the outcome in the future. If capitalism was made to lose profits to accommodate the needs of the people, then it would quickly seek ways to recoup. The scales are hardly likely to fall from its eyes. It is not about to shut up shop. This is not to say that capitalism will not make concessions in order to preserve its role. The case of the Ford Foundation and the massive "Black Lives Matter" (BLM) movement is a case in point.

Darren Walker (2015), president of the Ford Foundation, argues that capitalism is obliged to improve and strengthen the economic and political system. He oversaw a financial contribution of $100 million to the BLM. Many of the activists in BLM would describe themselves as anti-capitalist. The Ford Foundation do not share such an anti-capitalist perspective and assiduously work to limit any rise in class antagonisms. It begs the question as to what is meant by "strengthening the economic and political system"?

BLM represented something bigger than a simple identity political campaign. That something is best described as a social movement. Social movement activism, one might assume, as bigger, broader and potentially with a bigger agenda, might be that vehicle to unite ideas and people, to break the barriers of isolation and alienation that capitalism builds. It is abundantly clear that the state is relatively content to see protest. It "proves" that the system works. The phenomenon of the social movement, in an age of alienation, deserves some consideration.

Can social movement politics provide an answer?

As an extension of identity-based politics, social movement activism consciously seeks to broaden the scope for resistance. Social movement activism also seeks to build a sense of collective identity that is claimed to be broader than class identity. However, with a global working class hovering close to 3.5 billion, a "social movement" that is broader than class would be something to see. Traditional expressions of class-based identity are described as "old" social movements, which most usually take the form of trade union activism. The "new" forms have tended to carefully and deliberately move away from any overt identification with the working class.

The capacity for social movements to mobilise large numbers is obvious to anyone with eyes to see. The civil rights movement in the US in the 1960s, the anti-Vietnam, anti-nuclear, environment, the "occupy", anti-globalisation and anti-capitalist movements are all testimony to the success that these broad movements have in building a constituency. Sustaining constituencies becomes far more difficult. These movements often share things in common. They are inevitably political, in the sense that they make demands upon the state (Rootes 1997: 71) and they consciously seek to effect social change. Marco Guigni draws attention to some of the issues that these movements present:

> In their aim of changing the status quo, social movements face a fundamental dilemma. If they ask for short-term policy changes, they have a greater chance that such changes will occur, but they will not alter, in a fundamental way, existing structures and practices. If instead, movements demand long-term institutional changes, they will encounter more difficulties in realizing such changes...Social movements rarely alter political institutions and only under very restricted conditions (Guigni 1999: xxiv).

Social movement theory speaks of both reforming and revolutionary movements. Goodwin and Jasper (2009: 4) neatly explain the differences. They define a "revolutionary" movement as a social movement that actively seeks to overthrow the state, while a broader social movement, deemed to be a reforming instrument, "is a collective, organised, sustained, and non-institutional challenge to authorities, powerholders, or cultural beliefs and practices" (2009: 4). Needless to say, it is in the latter formation that social movements are most evident. There is a broadly accepted view that the purpose of social movements, and the political agendas they pursue, are aimed at moving society and institutions within that society to a less oppressive position. In effect the same problem as was discussed a little earlier in relation to identity politics and its appeal to the state and to capital remains.

Proponents of new social movement activism describe it as replacing older social movement forms. It should be reasonable, if that is the case, to begin to see some results. It would appear logical that there has been a greater degree of success with the new as opposed to the older "obsolete" movements. It also presupposes a fundamental difference in approach that is not always apparent.

The labour movement activism that the "new" social movement advocates suffered from a process of integration into the capitalist state structure. Ted Wheelwright (1953) traced the trajectory of the trade union movement and of state responses to union activism. He noted three phases in the relationship between the unions and the capitalist state. The first is one of hostility and attempts at suppression on the part of the state. The second is a position of tolerance but sees the state offering little cooperation to the unions. The third phase is one whereby the unions enter into a period of cooperation and partnership with the capitalist state. John Macionis (2007) in discussing newer forms of social movement activism outlines four stages that constitute the "life-cycle" of a social movement. These are success, co-optation, repression or establishment within the mainstream of society. There are striking similarities between his description and that of Wheelwright. That there are clear points of connection between "old" and "new" social movements indicate that problems associated with programme and intent remain unresolved. Activism, when constrained by integration into the very system that you are struggling against, is fraught with difficulties and frustrations.

In an alienated and alienating world, people are driven to

revolt and, when poorly led, to disillusionment and despair. The wheel turns and the problem of isolation is made that little bit more debilitating.

Of course, not everyone becomes engaged in political struggles against the state. If we were to canvas the people, we would find some who cling to a belief that things are as they should be. Others would recognise that things are bad and getting worse but hope that somehow it will get better. Still others are almost crushed beneath the weight that a broken system imposes upon them. Some will disengage in the hopes that they can escape, that their life can somehow be shored up against an alienating world. Regardless of where anybody might find themselves on this tragic spectrum, the simple and painful truth is that the downward spiral continues, but in every age, people have reacted to oppression and have sought to right wrongs. When they do the rage is real but so very often impotent. This, in our age, has been why social movement and identity politics have grown and for the reasons already outlined, withered on the vine.

Capitalist globalisation, as a direct response to a growing crisis within capitalism itself, and the rise of social movement politics have evolved together. Protests have been both national and international in scope. Some have adopted an "anti-capitalist" perspective. Others have focused on war, poverty or a range of social issues. Organisers have successfully been able to draw millions of people into protest and political action. The World Social Forum and the "Occupy" movement, among others, highlighted the discontent that many people were and are feeling. These actions assumed a growing significance as the globalisation of capitalism has progressed and are clearly a reaction against globalisation and capitalism. Political responses, either at a state level or at the level of an alienated people, frequently share a view that economic actions and outcomes can be separated from the globalisation of capitalism

– that capitalism and globalisation can be regarded as separate entities. Anti-globalisation becomes, for some, a euphemism for "deglobalisation". This has become more apparent since the anti-World Trade Organisation protests in Seattle in 1999 (Smith 2001: 1-20, Ayres 2001: 55-68). Some promote the idea that globalisation can be reversed, and that the nation-state is the vehicle through which such a reversal can be effected. Leslie Sklair (2002: 273-277) identifies a range of what he considers to be challenges to globalisation, including protectionism, social movements and the green movement. There has been conscious promotion of nationalism in the face of capitalist globalisation. Economic nationalism, political nationalism and the politics of populism are the results of this failed and failing capitalist system. Is populism, then, a representation of alienation on a mass scale?

Chapter 4

The pursuit of populism

The state is in some rather hot water. It does not and cannot offer any solution to the problems facing the people. It is not overstating things to say that there is a deep crisis of legitimacy and, as a consequence, and with the vacuum that this leaves, all manner of cracks are appearing. The cracks are deep and no amount of plaster, let alone paper, will make the building secure. For the state to function, there needs to be a semblance of legitimacy. It's all about a contract that is unconsciously entered into. While there are a range of interpretations, we can reasonably assume that legitimacy exists when there is an acceptance by the people of the rule and power of the state. In short, we give you the right to make decisions on our behalf, but expect that you provide us with security, peace and the right to a decent life. It is assumed that this contract will be without coercion, although the capitalist state has always operated as a coercive force. The point is that the coercive nature of the state in a class-based society has been masked. The people have accepted this state of affairs as a result of a long and highly successful ideological campaign, resulting in either the condition that Engels described as false consciousness or the Gramscian version of cultural hegemony.

The contract, if we can accept that such a contract ever existed, has been broken. The state and its institutions no longer deliver and, increasingly, the people have come to recognise this. They cannot but recognise this fact as reality daily hammers home the point. This, of course, simply means that people feel more and more alone and alienated from the very society, the very state that is supposed to exist to support them.

What this means for the state and capitalism and for the people who live and work in this reality is of intense importance.

The future of the capitalist state would seem to hang in the balance. The future of anti-capitalist movements similarly rests on how things play out. The alienation that Marx wrote of has become all pervasive and is now having a direct impact on the system itself. The issue of perceived or real "legitimacy" within the capitalist nation-state first needs to be examined, even if only briefly. This flows into the question of how things have unravelled. The how is intimately linked to the great and final contradiction of capitalism; the contradiction of an inevitable integration of global capitalism and the need to maintain the internal security that the state offers. What has transpired in the most recent period has been a rise in nationalist and populist sentiment. This has stemmed from the breakdown of capitalism and reactions to it. Fear of an unknown and unknowable future has found expression in the politics of nationalism and of populist rhetoric. The state has harnessed this sentiment that could so easily have been channelled into an anti-capitalist feeling and has promoted the twin issues of economic nationalism and political nationalism. Anything like a successful response to these issues can but lead us to a final question – what is to be done?

Living in a state of illegitimacy

The term legitimacy is often bandied about when talking of state theory. It is a term more often used by more powerful states when considering the merits of interfering in the business of weaker states. Then we have failed states or states that have lost legitimacy. Oddly enough a state never seems to use such terms in relation to itself, but should that really be surprising? While definitions abound, political scientists generally accept that legitimacy exists when there is an acceptance by the ruled that the rulers have political power and that this is both consensual and meets the needs of all concerned. Bruce Gilley offers a "definition of state legitimacy...as follows: a state is more legitimate the more that it is treated by its citizens as rightfully holding and exercising political power" (2006: 500).

It is a fact of life that the broad capitalist concept of democracy still holds the general support of the people or at least people still turn up in largish numbers to vote. While this is so, there is a general, across the board dissatisfaction with the whole process. Wike, Silver and Castillo (2019) in a report for the Pew Research Center show some disturbing trends. More than half of those surveyed across 27 countries feel dissatisfied with the democratic process, 60 per cent feel that elections do not change things for the better, and 61 per cent feel elected officials to be corrupt. There are some countries where the democratic process of voting is compulsory. The dissatisfaction levels in Australia, as an example, are rather telling. The Museum of Australian Democracy and the Institute for Governance and Policy Analysis at the University of Canberra have released findings from their joint research, *Trust and Democracy in Australia*, which shows that a worrying cultural shift has occurred in Australia. In 2007, 86 per cent of Australians were satisfied with the democratic process. By 2010 that figure had fallen to 72 per cent and then a collapse was recorded. In 2018, just 41 per cent of Australians still had any positive feeling for their democratic processes (Stoker, Evans and Halupka 2018).

Gilley's definition of what constitutes a legitimate society, and the reality of life for so many, points to the fact that something is terribly amiss. If democracy, or rather the democracy of capitalism, is losing support, then the idea of socialism is enjoying a corresponding boost. The vigorously anti-communist *Victims of Communism Memorial Foundation* (2019) conducts an annual survey of attitudes towards socialism, communism and collectivism. Its most recent findings were that 70 per cent of American millennials would vote for a socialist candidate. This follows Gallup polls that show a majority of young people are viewing the ideas of socialism in a favourable light. Such an idea, even just 10 years ago, would have been dismissed as little more than the mutterings of fantasists. We might spare a moment's thought for the members of the *Victims of Communism Memorial Foundation*. With each passing year the figures move in the wrong direction for them. It must be a depressing task, but it does go some way to show the difficulty that the state finds itself in, when all roads seem to lead to one conclusion; the system is losing its iron-clad hold on the minds of the citizenry. Legitimacy appears to be exiting via the back door.

It's not just that people are losing faith with this or that political party, or even that they are finding the whole electoral process to have little relevance. The question is why? Politicians are just as trustworthy or untrustworthy as they have ever been. They, either as individuals or as a collective, are being seen as symbols of the rot that has set in. In this case they become a focus for anger, rather than the actual cause of the growing misery. Living standards are not improving but, rather, are falling in just about every country. Health outcomes are deteriorating, educational institutions are failing our youth, despite heroic efforts on the part of doctors, nurses and teachers. More outcome, more productivity, more surplus value is being expected for less outlay. Wages are stagnating or shrinking, and, at the same time, there are ostentatious displays of wealth. More and more of the global wealth is being concentrated into fewer hands. The people see this and recognise the injustice, the inequality, and see little hope on the horizon.

Oxfam's 2018 Report revealed that 26 individuals own as much as the poorest 3.8 billion people on the planet (Oxfam 2018). Such statistics are ultimately meaningless. It is all but impossible to fully comprehend the enormity of these figures. What is less difficult to appreciate is that it does not make for a contented people anywhere. The vast majority of the super-rich come from a very few countries. We don't need to spell this out, and nor is it necessary to labour the point that there is a simmering resentment, bordering on open hostility, towards these people, or at least towards their loyal lieutenants who manage the state on their behalf.

Marxists have maintained since Marxism breathed its first that capitalism is based on antagonistic class relationships. They further maintain that the state exists to facilitate capitalism. For many decades, the state has been able to mask the exploitative nature of the economic system. This is growing less and less possible. The system lumbers on, not from any sense of "legitimacy" or any great sense of ownership by the people. It lumbers and lingers because the state, during the past couple of centuries, has made it really very difficult for people to imagine anything else. Why then is there suddenly such a feeling of despair and hopelessness in the air? The nation-state system that so many put such faith in has been shown to be wanting. Capitalism's primary business of securing profit has continued but it now has a tricky relationship with the state and vice versa. The intensification of globalised capitalist relations in the last few decades has led to many questions.

For so long now, the people have been told, and they believed what they heard, that it is in the warm embrace of the nation-state that we will find peace, security and harmony. Then, suddenly, a global economy appeared on the horizon. Its appearance seemed to coincide with a breakdown of the old ways. The system was no longer delivering. Jobs were disappearing. Someone or something had to be blamed. The reason for the dislocation and deepening crisis of fear and alienation was not globalisation, but capitalism's vain attempts to avoid a crisis that will dismember it.

There has to be someone or something to blame

Capitalism is clearly failing. This became apparent from the 1970s and the end of the "golden age" but the pace of collapse in just the last decade or so has been remarkable. Lives are being broken and yet capitalism is still not being specifically targeted, or at least not by enough of the people who are being made to suffer at its hands. This should not really be all that surprising. But even so, almost everyone acknowledges, almost instinctively, that something is wrong. It might be phrased differently, by different people. It might be "it's a different world now" or "that's how things are now" or "I just don't know". It might appear to be anger, or despair, or even indifference, but everyone knows that things are not as they should be. The good times are no longer rolling. It's got to be someone's fault. In time-honoured fashion blame has been laid at the door of the foreigner, the migrant, the refugee, the job stealer, the ones who are not quite like us. If it gets too difficult to justify, then there is always the one-size-fits-all, package-deal that is ready for blame: globalisation. It's big, can't easily be seen, but is an idea that can be made to sound scary and that fear can be taken on board without any need for deep analysis, or argument, and after all nobody quite seems to know how to identify it. In the case of globalisation, the fears can be easily understood. It is, after all, the end-point of capitalist integration, and is capitalism's last throw of the dice. However, finger pointing and blaming anything or anyone is a well-worn strategy, and well, let's be clear, if it has worked in the past, then why wouldn't it work now? If something is not going well, then the easiest, nearest "perceived" enemy will do. There is an obvious and painful reminder of the ease with which racism can be stirred up when the economy hits the rocks. Hitler had little trouble in tapping into a rich vein of fear and xenophobia. The economy was in ruins. Who to blame? It's the Jews, the Jewish bankers, the Bolsheviks, a conspiracy between the Jewish bankers and the Bolsheviks. We know who is responsible. The rest is easy. It didn't have to make sense. In the hands of the ideologues, it was made to "make sense". It's still going on, and, as with Hitler and Goebbels, the blame is placed variously on global institutions and individuals.

Since the explosion of capitalist globalisation from the 1970s, there have been so many enemies from which to choose. The borders of nation-states had become fetters to capitalist progress. Capitalism was moving offshore to escape the tendency for profits to fall. This has always been a nagging reality for capitalism, always present, sometimes lurking in the shadows and sometimes out in the open and staring capital in the face. New and cheaper labour sources were required. This was a move that had serious implications for the western working class and was met with a sense of resentment. "Our jobs have been stolen, our manufacturing industries have gone. Nothing's as it was or as it should be." When all is said and done, the state has spent countless hours over centuries convincing people that the nation is a unifying thing and that we have common interests that make us one, and then, suddenly, the rug seemed to have been pulled from under their feet.

A crime has been committed. Those who simply want to live in relative peace and quiet, to return to a time when the "contract" between the governed and the governing was intact have been let down. They will never be allowed to return to that real or imagined peace, as the state and capitalism continue to unravel. Those who seek a better future, free from capitalism and its insoluble contradictions, free from crisis and inequality, have similarly been cast adrift. This becomes acutely obvious when observed against the backdrop of the rapidity of capitalist globalisation. Everybody knows that things have gone terribly wrong but what is to be done? It all seems impossible. At least that is how it is presented. After all there are, supposedly, no other options.

As with all developments in capitalist relations, there are those who suffer. Why should we be surprised to discover that those who suffer most are the working class? The crisis in capitalism that precipitated globalisation from the 1970s saw a dramatic change in how capital arranged its affairs. Traditionally labour had been mobile and had to be. It simply went to where the jobs were. The history of the west has been a history of the immigrant, leaving home in search of a better life, somewhere where there was work. The crisis and subsequent speed up of capitalist globalisation saw this arrangement turned on its head. Capitalism now moves its operations to where the workers are to be found. Marxist theory argues that there is a tendency for profits to fall. Capital, and an increasingly global and integrated capital, moved to where the least expensive labour might be easily exploited. One consequence was a shattering of manufacturing in the developed countries. Another was the construction of an industrial working class in the developing world. Naturally there was ill-feeling, hostility and antagonism, but how was this to be expressed, and what outcomes might be expected?

Capitalism and globalisation have always been synonymous. Changes to capitalism have made this tendency towards globalisation more prominent and have directly led to conditions of heightened inequality. Globalisation has become a source of discontent and disquiet. Globalisation has been accompanied by accumulation of wealth and an intensification of poverty. As Marx so aptly put it, "accumulation of wealth at one pole is, therefore, at the same time accumulation of misery, agony of toil, slavery, ignorance, brutality, mental degradation, at the opposite pole" (Marx 1986b: 604).

The developed economies have seen a de-industrialisation, growing unemployment and a stagnation of wages that has led to increasing and obvious disparities between the extremely wealthy and the "rest". There have been, of course, many claims that globalisation has led to millions in the developing world being brought out of poverty. This may be the case, or at least it is on a superficial telling of the story. The developing world has seen and is seeing a dramatic rise in an industrial working class. This means a relatively quick rise from abject poverty to, well, poverty. While this may be lauded the fact remains that exploitation remains and the relativities between rich and poor not only remain but increase. The new working class in the developing world also get to enjoy the deep sense of alienation that goes hand in hand with life under capitalism.

Globalisation, then, loomed large in the thinking of the working class and the increasingly "squeezed" middle class. For many in the west the question appeared to be, how best to resist globalisation, and how to promote an anti-globalist or anti-capitalist agenda? For some it became, and remains, a question of reversing the tendency of capitalist globalisation: to "de-globalise". For others, it is to present globalisation as a political issue that can be somehow separated from over-riding economic considerations. What needs to be remembered is that there is an inseparable unity between economic globalisation and capitalism. Globalisation, in itself, is not the cause of the misery that anti-globalists depict. It is capitalism that is the ultimate source of that misery.

The new century dawned and with it the endless "war on terror". Barak Obama, while still president of the US, addressed officer recruits at West Point. His message was broadcast around the world but received little criticism. He was, of course, marketed as the "good guy" president. In his speech he bluntly stated that, "The United States will use military force, unilaterally if necessary, when our core interests demand it—when our people are threatened, when our livelihoods are at stake, when the security of our allies is in danger...International opinion matters, but America should never ask permission to protect our people, our homeland, or our way of life." The dominant world power "should never ask permission" and nor have they. Millions of refugees have been the result. The fact that the foreign policy endeavours of the US and its allies were at the root of the refugee crisis has been conveniently overlooked. The waves of refugees, asylum seekers, illegal immigrants – pick a pejorative, any pejorative – added fuel to the fires of fear and anxiety that stalked the west. Capitalism and its public relations experts skilfully managed to avoid being held to account for its failure. It was, after all, "globalisation" that was to blame. It remained a formless, shapeless but foreign enemy. The added beauty was that globalisation is equally "foreign" to anyone anywhere in the world. It was globalisation that was to blame and not capitalism or capitalist globalisation. They are very clever.

The blame game has been successful, but like everything else, is fraught with contradictory possibilities. Capitalism is increasingly integrated. The borders of nation-states are encumbrances to its growth. The nation-state must maintain peace, stability and order for capitalism to grow. The people are seeing that the state no longer provides for their needs. There is a call to return to simpler times, but time and the economics of capitalism do not have a reverse gear. There are calls for nationalist revivals, for economic nationalism, trade wars and protectionism. If these calls were to be successful, then capitalism would disintegrate and the world would, in all likelihood, be plunged into war. Capitalist globalisation, like capitalism itself, is not the answer and nor is nationalism. Nationalism can only separate people from another and foster fear and intolerance. It feeds on fear and insecurity with the result being greater fear and greater insecurity. What then of the place of nationalism in our sea of anxiety?

Can nationalism be anti-capitalism?

Joseph Stiglitz (2006), former chief economist at the World Bank, described how the developed economies were shaping the new globalised relations to best suit their interests. Such authoritative voices gave heart and impetus to anti-capitalist theorists and activists. Walden Bello (2013), for instance, argues that "deglobalisation" is becoming a very real option. Central to this idea is the need to promote and revitalise national economies. It is a common enough call and one that fits with much of the rhetoric of the right, except, of course, the idea of pursuing anti-capitalist goals. Other anti-globalisation thinkers, including Dani Rodrik (1997), describe what they see as a backlash against the more destructive consequences of globalisation. There is often a sense of excitement that gets generated, even when it is not always warranted. Brian Burgoon (2013) goes so far as to claim that the rise in social inequality that accompanies globalisation can be used to move political parties to effective anti-globalist action. There is a problem with all this. It separates, or tries to separate, two inseparable things.

We need to remember that globalisation is not a physical entity. It cannot be moved here or there on a whim. It is a process and a continuation of capitalist relations that have been developing ever since capitalism first emerged. Official governmental policies may come and go, but the process of capitalist globalisation is an irreversible one. Capitalism has been moving in this direction since the industrial revolution. National borders have no meaning for capital. Regardless of what someone might want, or wish for, no matter how much an individual might long to see the process move into reverse, they risk being characterised, as Marx and Engels (1977: 63-64) characterised petty-bourgeois socialism's desire to hold back the historical processes, as being, at best, utopian. What is fascinating is that nationalism which has been used time and again to promote the ideas of the state and therefore the interests of capitalism can, with the flourish of a pen, miraculously become an ideological tool to fight capitalist globalisation. With such magic in the air, it is clear that we do live in strange and wondrous times.

Two factors can be seen at play. We need to remember, firstly, that capitalism, although bound to globalise, is not, of itself, monolithic. Sections of capital are invariably in conflict with one another. What propels one section might spell disaster for another. Globalisation, while dominating capitalist relations, has an impact on the remnants of local or national capital. More importantly, however, is the second factor. That is the power and control that nation-states have exerted and continue to exert. This is most obviously reflected in the power rivalries between the US and China. Neither is prepared to be anything but the dominant player on the world stage. Individual capitalist corporations may nominally be based here or there, but they exist largely beyond the bounds of the nation-state. So, either the nation-state must disappear, and individual capitalists find a way to manage the globe, or the nation-state seeks to exert its influence. Survival is an intensely strong motivating force. What we are witnessing is a repeat of what happened when globalisation met nation-state resistance in the lead up to WWI and again in the 1930s when, as Trotsky described it, the demand was "back to the national hearth" (Trotsky 1956) despite this being ultimately impossible.

So, there is an almost inevitable backlash and it is seen clearly in the work of the anti-globalisation theorists. What ought to be a puzzling and disturbing thing for these writers is that while the first set of worried activists were, broadly speaking, of the left, the newer breed are decidedly more right-wing. This "big switch" (Horner, Schindler, Haberly and Aoyama 2018) describes the motivations behind Brexit and the rise of Trump, but the British and Americans are not alone among major political players to embrace a right-wing anti-globalisation stance. The great contradiction between global capitalism and the nation-state has manifested itself in some rather disturbing political outcomes in the most recent period. Political parties that would have lurked in the shadows just a decade ago are now significant forces across many European states. Avowedly right-wing parties in Austria, Belgium, the Czech Republic, Denmark, Estonia, France, Germany, Hungary, Italy, Poland, Switzerland have all shown significant growth. The right are more and more occupying positions of influence in the various parliaments across the world. The extreme right, the mainstream conservative parties and increasingly the parties of social democracy are all promoting economic and political programmes that are designed to reinforce the sense of nation, one-ness and some fading or imagined image of a glorious past that can be miraculously resurrected. There are anti-immigrant, xenophobic policies, and calls for a "return" to economic nationalism. In a desperate attempt to shore up belief and faith in a system that is no longer capable of delivering, these patriotic fanfares serve to lock in a sense of fear.

What is of some significance in all this is the common ground that the extreme right and the mainstream political forces now occupy. To say that it is disturbing is an understatement. The arguments surrounding tariffs and trade wars are a case in point. Economic nationalism, most simply described as economic policies that favour the home nation but almost inevitably at the expense of other nations, has been an easy package to sell. We have already had the marketing of the state for centuries promoting the near mystical qualities of the nation and of its importance. If we are going to make America, or Britain, or Australia or any other nation "great", then we need to do several things. We must make the people's chests swell with pride, we must promote "our" economy over "theirs" and we must ignore the fact that while we are busy making "us" great, so too are "they" performing the same chest-beating rituals. We can only be great if someone else becomes less great. Another problem with this is that historically it has led us to slaughter each other.

This century has, thus far, been marked by a rise in antagonisms between capitalist powers as protectionist policies begin to invade state-to-state relationships. The World Trade Organisation (2016) and the former Chairman of the US Federal Reserve, Ben Bernanke (2006), had warned against the slide into protectionism and of its potential ramifications for the global economy.

What is worrying is the dangerous precedents that can be seen from just over a century ago. Then the world economy was integrating rapidly. Various capitalist states sought to stop and reverse this unavoidable trend to globalisation. Economic nationalism led directly to political nationalism, militarism and war. National states behave in this manner both as a response to economic downturn and also as a means of accommodating and soothing the fears and concerns of domestic populations that are forced to live with a failing economic system.

Nationalism has proven to be a most resilient phenomenon and one that has been carefully and consciously promoted and nurtured by capitalism. The use of emotive symbolism and the ethos of nationalism is a deliberate act of social control in order to manipulate the people and to maintain some form of social order. Nationalism and, in this context, economic nationalism pit one nation against another and by implication one worker against another There are implicit dangers for national economies and for the working class in such a perspective. The working class, under protectionist conditions, is encouraged, at the very least, to view the working class of "competing" nations as rivals for jobs. This is often combined with appeals to freedom and the danger of a loss of freedom. It's not as though the working class or anyone else needs any more stress, or fear to be heaped on their plates.

The promotion of nationalist perspectives echoes political and economic debates dating back a century when free traders and protectionists struggled for dominance in the lead up to World War I. What is fundamentally different in this twenty-first century version of the debate is that protectionism and economic nationalism are even less viable options. Capitalist globalisation, as unpalatable as that may be, will continue as long as capitalism reigns. To seek an alternative vision evokes Marx and Engels' response to utopianism and its call to an "earlier" political and economic foundation and to turning back clocks (Marx and Engels 1977).

The attempts to turn back the clocks or, Canute-like, to order back the tides are going on and are at the very heart of populist politics. It is within populism that we can see a dangerous rise in fear and anxiety as we learn to distrust that awkward "other".

Getting to know populism

There is always a new buzz-word, phrase or term that is "the" word of the moment. A journalist may pick up on something said, it will be repeated and hey-presto, you can't move for it. The word "populism" is a term that not only burst onto the pages and into our consciousness in the early years of this century, but it has tended to stay there. The frustrating thing about this term is that it has been used first to denigrate and then to praise, almost simultaneously. I had the dubious pleasure of attending a conference a couple of years back devoted to the concept of populism. The great majority of speakers were fierce in their condemnation of populism, but in the next room a panel of speakers waxed lyrical about the beauty of "left" populism, and of how it would save South America and the world. Back in the "real world" there are more and more voices that sing the praises of populism as a means of saving democracy. So, in this confused and confusing world, anything goes and everybody can claim to be equally correct.

"A populism focused on the renewal of democracy may indeed be an unsettling prospect, but if this is what is needed to halt its slow downward spiral into the void, it will be a price worth paying" enthuses Simon Tormey (2019: 129). Democracy, after all, is one of those things that must be defended at all costs. To speak otherwise is to commit a terrible blasphemy. Capitalism informs the state. The state is the state of the ruling ideology: capitalism. Democracy ensures that we, the people, are convinced that things are working and that all is as it should be. The circle is complete and within the circle we are embraced and secure. Populism, when presented as something of a saviour of democracy and therefore of the political and economic system itself, must be a good thing. Such an unlikely picture is given to us by Manuel Anselmi (2018) when he argues that populism is a very definite option for democracy.

Sometimes, as with our conference speakers, "good" or "bad" populisms can be found. It is comforting that we can pick a reality that best fits with how we want to view the world. For those who see themselves as "progressive", Trump is a dangerous populist. Conservatives are of one mind in their view that Venezuelan president Maduro is a dangerous populist. The beautiful thing about it all is that neither side appears to see the obvious irony. David McKnight (2018) differentiates between variations of positive and negative populism. There is nothing wrong in any of this, but it needs to be borne in mind that "populism is not a corrective to liberal democracy in the sense of bringing politics 'closer to the people'...as is sometimes claimed. But it can be useful in making it clear that parts of the population really are unrepresented" (Muller 2016: 58). Muller's point is worth considering. People are more and more "unrepresented" and feel this. The populist, the ideologue, can and is manipulating this sense of alienation.

Populism is, at the end of the day, an ideology. It shares with any ideology a set of views and perceptions. Its adherents believe in these ideas. Regardless of whether the populism is of the left or right there are three essential features that mark out populism. There is an appeal to the "people". There is a denunciation of the "elite" and a demand that politics should be an expression of the "general will" (Mudde and Kaltwaser 2017). Now all this sounds rather appealing. It sounds as if it is calling to just about all in society, but on closer inspection, it is not. Determining the "will" of the people is always going to be tricky. Hitler knew the will of the people; Stalin understood the will of the people. Which people? Which section of society? Is it ethnically-based, nationally-based, is it divisive? Does it seek to challenge and fundamentally change society? Does it seek to make the system work when the system is broken? What happens when a left populism such as Syriza in Greece comes to power and then proceeds to enforce the same austerity measures it had denounced as the work of the "elites"? What happens when a right populism such as Trump's presidency drives the world to the brink of war? Populism is a tantalising thing. It is slippery. It seems to be able to be all things to all people and ultimately equates to nothing. As Cas Mudde described the theory, "populism is a thin-centred ideology that considers society to be ultimately separated into two homogenous and antagonistic groups, 'the pure people' versus the 'corrupt elite' and which argues that politics should be the expression of the *volunte generale* (general will) of the people" (2004: 543).

If we can accept that it is capitalism that is the problem, then it is not too difficult to accept that anything that diverts attention from that simple fact simply delays facing up to reality. Populism, in whatever form it is presented, almost inevitably offers immediate national responses to what are effectively global problems. It can't really do anything else. In focusing on an often-amorphous elite, broader understandings of class and internationalism become blurred. The issue of leadership quickly asserts itself. Discontent does not go away. Populist arguments might corral and seem to organise discontent into action, but these actions have a nasty habit of dissipating. "Left" and "right" expressions of disaffection frequently appear to merge. The "enemy" in such ideological construction can be foreign workers, economic competition from other nations, or an ill-defined globalisation.

The willingness of broad sections of the people, the working class and middle class, to embrace populist ideas and to throw their weight behind the ideologues espousing these simplistic ideas is a very real indication of a people on the move. The people, aware of the dislocation and misery that befalls them, are giving every indication that they are rejecting the politics of the capitalist state. They are giving every indication that they are looking for ways to break the *status quo* and to find a way out of the nightmare and struggle that epitomises life in late capitalism. This becomes a fearful moment for the state, unless it can pull more rabbits from its ideological hat. The state, then, in time-honoured fashion seeks to channel discontent, to shore up support and to enable the system to survive for just a little longer.

The state learns to embrace populism

Populism ought to be a worrying thing for the state. Its theorists and, importantly, its supporters rail against the "elite". The state apparatus, one would have to accept, is the embodiment of the political elite. It is the state, after all, that calls the shots. Populism, in any telling of the theory, demands a "bottom-up" approach to politics. The state and populism, one might imagine, are sworn enemies. Something rather odd seems to have happened along the way. Populism has begun to be legitimised. While this might be odd, it is not entirely unusual.

Capitalism and the state have a long and somewhat distinguished career in co-opting ideas and organisations to serve their version of the "greater good". The organisations of the working class are a prime example. It was briefly discussed earlier how the union movement became legitimised and integrated into the state through a three-phase process of first, hostility, then tolerance and finally cooperation and partnership. A consequence of this integration, as far as the working class is concerned, has been a loss of independence. This is by no means a recent development in state and class relations. "Capitalism is less and less willing to reconcile itself to the independence of trade unions. It demands of the reformist bureaucracy...that they become transformed into its political police before the eyes of the working class" (Trotsky 1972: 11). Trotsky wrote those words in 1926. How is it not possible to see similarities in how populism is being regarded?

A "bottom-up" movement can, of course, be a little troubling if you want to maintain control of things. Slowly, the language begins to change. We begin to see the promotion of the idea that populism might have an "up-side". Damon Acemoglu and James Robinson, writing in the influential American *Foreign Policy* magazine (2019), describe two potential states – the despotic and the impaired – and that between these two runs a narrow corridor. It is in this corridor, they assert, that liberty can rise. Speaking specifically about the American experience, they argue that despite all of the negatives associated with populism, its xenophobia and its nationalism, this very bottom-up mobilisation has the capacity to pull the US back from the edge. What we appear to be witnessing is the legitimisation of populism, the accommodation of the state to populist rhetoric and the integration of the disempowered into the apparatuses of state that first disempowered them. It's a neat bit of conjuring.

This idea is given credence by recent research from the Tony Blair Institute for Global Change. As at March 2019, 68 per cent of G20 GDP was controlled by governments that could be described as populist. The same research shows that in 2018 there were 20 elected state leaders who were described as populist (Kyle and Gultchin 2019). What the research is less clear about is that there are more and more instances of mainstream parties adopting elements of populist ideas. The case of Australia, for instance, shows both governing and opposition parties taking on board policies that are clearly populist in nature.

The rapid rise of populist politics has sent political theorists into something of a spin. How should they regard this turn of events? Ignoring them is clearly not an option. Elections prove this to be the case. Up to a quarter of voters across OECD states are now registering support for these groups that claim to be speaking for the people and not the elites. This figure means large electoral success and large parliamentary representations, and this means entry into government, either formally as coalition partners or less formally but equally importantly ensuring that legislation succeeds or fails. This has led many analysts to ask some questions, although there ought to be enough evidence to show how things will most likely play out. The question that plays on their minds is whether the "new" forces will remain "responsive" to their constituencies, or become "responsible" and therefore promote the needs of the state and, necessarily, capital? Of special concern is how the *status quo* within a country so placed will play out should the populists remain true to their colours? Such a situation might risk stability at home and affect relations with other states. Conversely, accommodation with the interests of the state, and therefore the "elites", will lead to demoralisation and dissatisfaction (Plescia, Kritzinger and De Sio 2019). There really needs to be no need for such anxiety. These political movements are motivated by reaction to what they see as injustice or disempowerment. What is lacking is a programme for fundamental change and, like single-issue movements, identity movements, social movements are subject to confusion and dissipation.

Populism exists because people feel themselves to be cast aside. This anger can and has been manipulated by ideologues and can equally be manipulated by the state. Such energy must be channelled, or it is energy too easily spent. Trotsky, describing the necessity of political leadership, remarked that "without a guiding organisation the energy of the masses would dissipate like steam not enclosed in a piston box" (Trotsky 1965: 17). Populist sentiment is channelled into the mainstream political structures. This seems logical. What is worrying is that the mainstream is showing a greater propensity to move further to the right. There are distinct fascistic tendencies beginning to manifest themselves across many western states.

While this may be the case for right-wing populist movements, surely the left variants offer some hope? Sadly, it has not turned out that way. Much of the left became rather animated by left-populist movements of Syriza in Greece and Podemas in Spain. Syriza came to power as a protest against European Union austerity measures but, after 4 years of further austerity, it was replaced by a conservative government. The 2019 Spanish elections saw the rise of the fascistic Vox party, and significantly Podemas entered into a coalition with the Spanish Socialist Party. Before the election, the socialist leader remained standoffish, dismissing the populists. The Podemas leader, Pablo Iglesias, in a statement after the election, commented that "we will be a minority in a government with the PSOE in which we will face many limits and contradictions, and we will have to give up on many things". Whether these are the words of retreat and opportunism or of political realism is very much in the eye of the beholder, but it indicates that the state, ultimately, has little to fear from left populism. It's a problem that pivots around questions of programme, of what political objectives are determined and how these objectives are to be achieved.

A final example of the madness in which we find ourselves is in how all sorts of ostensibly bitter enemies can become bosom allies. New solidarities are forged. Far right leader Nigel Farage, ex-Trotskyist leader Claire Fox and former doyen of the UK Labour left George Galloway now sing each other's praises. In the midst of all this madness, there can be only one winner, albeit a temporary winner. The going has certainly become tough and for more than a few, the pressure seems to have become too much.

There is much that can be learned from all of this. Capitalism is in deep trouble and shows no capacity to escape its own existential contradictions. The state as facilitator of capitalist relations is barely holding things together. Traditional political expressions, or those of bourgeois politics, have all but lost their legitimacy. The people, the working class and, increasingly, the middle class are becoming the victims of this collapse. The working class has been stretched beyond all that is acceptable.

Chapter 5

A world aflame

This book was written between 2019 and 2020. It was a time of tumult. Across nations and continents there was open revolt. The streets were filled with angry men and women. The state response was the same everywhere. Tear gas, water cannon, baton charges and instances of live fire were used to push the people back into their accepted and acceptable state of acquiescence. Different observers had different takes on the events of 2019. For some, it was a fearful anarchy and an end of order. For others it heralded imminent and positive change. The year 2019 was quite a year. Whether it marks the end of civilisation or the beginning of something new is dependent on many things; both objective and subjective. The objective conditions – the breakdown of capitalism and the breakdown of state legitimacy – are there for all to see. Whatever happens in the immediate future will not change those objective conditions that demand action. The subjective conditions – the readiness of the people to make change a reality, a leadership that has a clear vision of the way forward, and an acceptance, on the part of the people, that this leadership speaks for them – are less clear, although the fog certainly does appear to be lifting.

The year and its events did not spring from a vacuum. The entire century has been one of seething resentment toward a system that doesn't work, and which no longer even pretends to care. The year 2020 would certainly appear to be a watershed moment, but it would be the height of foolishness to predict what will happen a month, a year or a decade from today. The only thing that can be said for certain is that change is in the air, it is on the agenda, and capitalism is driving people to make the choice for change. There is a quote that is often attributed to Lenin. "There are decades where nothing happens; and there are weeks where decades happen." The history of the Marxist movement is a testament to the truth of that quote, regardless of who did say it. We seem to be living in a moment where decades are happening in weeks.

Everybody, it seems, has the answer, or at least an answer. What the world has been witnessing does need exploring in some detail. A range of questions need looking at. Why has the world exploded now, at this moment in time? How has it been explained and why so many "explanations"? What does it all mean for capital, the state and for the working class? If a Pandora's box has been opened, then what will be the result? Is the curtain rising on the last act of the tragedy called capitalism?

Marxists maintain that theirs is a view based in science. The claim is made that the trajectory of capitalism is very much a law-driven thing. The history of human, economic and political development indicates a movement of social and class forces. There will be no launching into a treatise on historical materialism, but at the same time, it is perhaps appropriate to offer a little background.

Can Marxist theory take away some of the fear?

If we look at the world, and at the turmoil and anger that is evident everywhere, then it needs to be able to be explained. If it cannot be explained, then there is nothing but despair. It is simply not good enough to say there is a crisis, that capitalism can't deliver, that this or that individual, group of individuals, government or the economic system has got it wrong. Yes, all of these, from the individual to the entire system is at fault, but how and why are we in this mess? Marxism was created to explain things and to offer a way to change things. It's what it is for. The good news is, for the sake of our discussion, explaining this element of Marxist theory, historical materialism, is nowhere near as complicated as some would have it.

Engels, in outlining what historical materialism was all about, argued that:

The materialist conception of history starts from the proposition that the production of the means to support human life and, next to production, the exchange of things produced, is the basis of all social structure; that in every society that has appeared in history, the manner in which wealth is distributed and society divided into classes or orders is dependent upon what is produced, how it is produced, and how the products are exchanged. From this point of view, the final causes of all social changes and political revolutions are to be sought, not in men's brains, not in men's better insights into eternal truth and justice, but in changes in the modes of production and exchange (1986: 411).

In other words, society is driven by economics and economics is arranged along class lines. How economic structures are arranged determines how society operates.

Human and societal development has moved through a number of developmental stages. Marxist theory describes these as being primitive communism or hunter-gatherer society, the ancient mode of production or slave society, feudalism, bourgeois or capitalist society, and in the future, into a lower form of communism or the dictatorship of the proletariat, and then a higher form of communism, where the state "withers" away. Critics of Marxism and of an historical materialist view of things are quick to point out that this construction is largely euro-centric in nature and that large parts of the world have not necessarily conformed to such a neat developmental package. Whether this criticism is entirely valid, given the fact that there are precious few peoples on earth whose lives are not framed by the last stage of development before socialism, is open to debate. Even so, Marx was careful to point out that what he was presenting was a guideline to historical research. However, it remains important to note, as Lenin observed, that Marx "studied the birth of a new society out of the old, and the forms of the transition from the latter to the former" (1977c: 272, emphasis in the original).

What is significant in this "guideline" is that the earliest stage, "primitive communism", is marked by the fact that there was no surplus being produced and, as a result, no-one was being exploited. Classes did not yet exist. Each successive stage is marked by a development of the productive forces and the development of classes that either exploited or were exploited. Each stage of development had limitations beyond which further growth or an ability to remain "afloat" simply became impossible. Each formulation was overcome by the next, but not without intense struggle. Nobody, it seems, wishes to go gently into any good night. This is so obviously and transparently the case at the moment. Capitalism, as the current stage in human development, is patently reaching the end of its use-by-date. This is mirrored within the capitalist world. Individual capitalist enterprises come and go, economies and nations rise and fall. We are witnessing this today as China assumes an ascendency, while the US begins to decline as the dominant economic player.

The US and other nation-states may call China a "communist" state as loudly and as often as they can. It does not alter the fact that the Chinese economy is capitalist. Its rise threatens rival capitalist states, even as they all share an overarching global integration of capitalist relationships. It makes for interesting, if extremely dangerous, times. States rise and fall. Empires come and go. And so it is with the coming to the fore of capitalism, its rise as a global force and its imminent collapse and breakdown.

As capitalist crisis deepens, Marxism assumes even more importance as a means of analysis. What remains significant is, as Engels put it, "two great discoveries, the materialistic conception of history and the revelation of the secret of capitalistic production through surplus value, we owe to Marx. With these discoveries, socialism became a science. The next thing was to work out all its details and relations" (1986: 411).

An understanding of these "details" and "relations" is important. Knowing what is going on and why things are happening as they are can only be to the good. We are pulled this way and that. People are afraid. Nobody seems to be in charge. The working class and sections of the middle class have, over so many decades, been encouraged to pledge their allegiance to a system that was in charge of things and then suddenly, no-one was.

Why has the world exploded now, at this moment in time?

Explosive images filled screens and newspapers throughout 2019. They were images of people on the march and no longer prepared to soak up assurances by the state that all is well and that at most a few minor tweaks will set things to rights. What was particularly noteworthy about these events was that they crossed continents, and cultures, while having such obvious similarities. Any one of the risings ought to have been enough to signal that there was a crisis. However, it was not just one country. Haiti, Chile, Bolivia, Colombia, Lebanon, Iraq, Iran and Hong Kong were all shrouded in tear gas. Hundreds were killed. What appeared to be "inconsequential" triggers – phone costs, train ticket price rises and the like – were simply tipping points for an angry population. Significantly it was the working class in these countries that began to play a prominent role. Equally significant was a common problem that faced them all. That problem was a lack of programme and of leadership. The anger did not go away, but without clear goals there can really be no clear destination.

Those pictures of thousands of people on the streets are glossed over, given a brief, half-hearted analysis and the news machine moves on. But they are images that cannot be easily ignored. Worker unrest in the US, India, across Europe, in China are easier to ignore. They don't quite have the same selling power for the media. That does not make them any less relevant. Far from it. Strikes in the US are at a 32-year high. Workers are regularly defying their union leaderships in order to continue struggles. The same scenario is being presented in so many countries. Workers in Canada, the UK, Belgium, France, just about everywhere, are beginning to recognise their collective potential. In India there have been general strikes with tens of millions of workers in manufacturing, transport, banks, public services taking part. Class is once more becoming important. To put the lie to the absurd claims that China has anything to do with socialism, there have been record numbers of strikes. The bulk of these have been in privately-owned enterprises. These strikes, up 36 per cent in a year, have been vigorously crushed by the state.

The world, it seems, is aflame. Why now? Why this moment in time? What will happen next and can anyone say, with any degree of certainty, what is in the wind? This is where it helps to have at least a bit of Marx on hand. A little over a hundred years ago, Marxism split into two divergent camps, never to come together again. Now there has been many a split since then but this was decisive. Among the issues that divided Marxists was the question of whether capitalism was in some way able to regulate itself, or whether it was destined to break down , under the weight of its various contradictions. While this debate raged, a closely related question of how to deal with capitalism and of the path to socialism was being thrashed out. It was the famous reform or revolution polemic.

It is not necessary to go into detail about these debates. Those who believed that socialism could come, gradually, incrementally and through reforms seemed to win the day. Marxism was renounced by these forces. The result was the rise of social democratic, or labour parties. While enjoying the weight of numbers and winning the support of the vast majority of the working class, capitalism has remained unchallenged. Any reforms were, by and large, rolled back over time and today these same parties are loyal supporters of the state and of capitalism. Capitalism, it would seem, has been able to roll with the punches and survive. Those who maintained that Marxism, and a classical interpretation of Marxism, was the way forward have had a difficult time. On the one hand, Stalinism did its level best to destroy the idea, and capitalism, aided and abetted by Stalinism, was happy to lend a hand.

This brings us back to the here and now. It looks rather as though the breakdown theory of capitalism has more than a little going for it. Even the most casual glance will reveal that it is in deep crisis and has no more tricks up its sleeve, apart from fascism or war. Even so, neither of these options could resolve any of the problems that capitalism faces and has been facing since day one. What we seem to be witnessing are the "end days" of an economic formation. Historical materialism describes these formations. Each succeeding one was forced upon its predecessor. The feudal lords and absolute monarchs did not simply put up the shutters and go into a quiet and dignified retirement. Economic conditions demanded that they left the stage. The rising bourgeois forces, through revolutions, made sure that this was the case. The time was right. Those that had the most to gain from such actions became the new ruling class. It's just how things roll.

The time is right for the rule of capital to come to an end. Economic conditions demand that this be so. Class matters and in this case, the case that is being played out in our time, it is the working class that will assume the leading role. Why it is happening at this moment in time is simple. The elastic can stretch only so far. Capitalism has reached the end of that stretch. So, if it is as simple as that, and the time is right for change, why has it not happened? Again, it is necessary to use just a bit of Marxist theory.

This "revolutionary" change requires two conditions to occur. Productive forces need to be highly developed and the working class and its allies must assume political power. In other words, what is required is a coming together of objective and subjective conditions for fundamental change. The objective conditions for change are well in place and have been for some time. The subjective factors – the class consciousness of the working class as revolutionary subject armed with a resolute political leadership – remain in embryonic form. What is obvious from the recent upheavals, strike activity and outbursts of anger, is that the working class is beginning to become aware of the power it possesses. What is lacking is leadership. Trotsky, in one sentence, summed up this situation. "The world political situation as a whole is chiefly characterized by a historical crisis of the leadership of the proletariat" (1977: 1). He had more to say than this, but it shows the simplicity and depth of the task before those who would seek a better future. Until such time as those "subjective" factors align, then there will be disappointments aplenty. However, from each disappointment comes another step along a learning curve. Reality and disappointment can be a great teacher.

The state and its media, unfortunately, do not seek Marxist analyses. Their business is, after all, to maintain a feeling that all is well, even when it is patently obvious that all is not well. But then this ought not to be all that surprising. Just 10 days before Berlin fell to the Soviet army at the end of WWII, Joseph Goebbels wrote his last editorial for the German paper *Das Reich*, calling for "resistance at any price". He could not admit that the end had come. The US, today, cannot accept that their day in the sun is at an end and that a rival capitalist power, China, is eclipsing them. Nobody, it seems, likes to hear unpalatable truths. The expressions of anger, frustration and of a growing awareness of capitalism's failure is similarly treated by the state and the media.

How has it been explained and why so many "explanations"?

The visual images of rebellion that filled our screens in 2019 were dutifully analysed and probed by the media. There was plenty of the "what" of the events, and to a limited degree, and sometimes in a contradictory way, the "why". It might be a little unfair to expect that the media should spend much time on explaining why, at this moment in time, the anger of millions should spill over. Traditionally the media, as an institution of the state, has had a role to play. Sometimes their relationship with the state may become strained, but essentially, they play an established role and serve a particular purpose. When it is necessary to give an opinion as to why such events happen, the analysis is often limited. This was especially the case during the crisis times of 2019.

To fully prove the point would mean another book, but just a few examples are worth looking at. Academics are certainly paying attention. Peter McPhee (2019) poses the question, "in a world of upheaval, why aren't today's protests leading to revolutions?" His special area of expertise is the French Revolution and he frequently compares and contrasts the revolutions in France, Russia, America, China and England. Turning his attention to the events of 2019, he rightly points out that mass protests fail if they are unable to create unity around core objectives. This is in keeping with the idea that leadership and programme are indispensable elements. He then lays the blame for the levels of rage on the "democratic deficit". By this he means that the reforms around the globe in the 1990s, coinciding with economic globalisation, have had "uneven" social outcomes. To his credit, McPhee recognises the growth of inequality as a factor, but the democratic reforms that he describes do not take into account what is happening across long-established democratic states, the palpable anger aimed against capital itself, and the growth in working class militancy. The focus remains on the upheavals that produce the better images for the screen. The media's "analysis" is rather telling.

The coverage of events that rocked Chile, as an example, are worth considering. Sebastian Boyd (2019) writing for *The Washington Post* points out that Chile is a most prosperous economy, while acknowledging that Chileans have long been frustrated at growing income inequality. Boyd explains that there was no leadership, but that this became more of a problem for the government than for those demanding change, as there was nobody for the government to negotiate with, which is an extraordinary take on the reality of the protests. Boyd then grapples with the "why" question. He seems honestly puzzled. Chile, he informs us, had done much to reduce poverty but in the same breath tells us that its inequality rate is one of the highest among OECD countries. The problem, in *The Washington Post's* estimation, is that political parties have done a "poor job" of channelling discontent. There is an assumption that if the government had been able to find a decent scapegoat, and "channelled" discontent, then all would be well! Such is the level of analysis in one of the world's more prestigious newspapers.

If we move from Chile to Iraq, then the media offers similarly limited coverage. The background to the eruption had different roots, and yet a common factor was an angry working class – demanding jobs and social services. The focus of the anger was able to be very quickly shifted towards Iran, which is of itself interesting. *Deutsche Welle* (DW) (2019) sought to "open up" and explain the crisis in Iraq. Their reporting of events accepted that anger over living standards was a major contributing factor and that "social frustration" was the primary issue. They were referring to mass unemployment, a lack of social services and monumental corruption. The DW reporters asked how it is that such a wealthy country can be so poor. They accept that the US and its war against Iraq has more than a little to do with things and that it is one of the more outrageously corrupt states on the planet. The fact that anger was able to be so easily channelled into anti-Iranian sentiment and along with it the fall-back position of nationalism has also been described. However, what was not so clear, in their report, as with the Chilean case, was why it erupted at that particular moment in history. Few reporters appear inclined to draw comparisons between the two countries, or indeed the anger in Iran, Lebanon or Columbia, let alone the working class in the developed western states.

Similar reportage, by similar media outlets, all seemed to say the same things, or rather leave unsaid the same things. Wherever possible mention of the growing role of the working class was downplayed. The common denominator, growing social inequality, a crisis in living standards, and a general despair that is being felt across the world as capitalism spirals into something of a death-spin, has to be kept from the consumers of media. To do otherwise would be unthinkable. The institutions of the state, whatever they might be, cannot be expected to act against the interests of the state.

Despite the very best interests of those engaged with maintaining a foggy ideological atmosphere, it is increasingly clear that the people are becoming aware that things have gone astray. This by no way means that the working class has become, as if at a stroke, class conscious. Far from it. Returning to Marx and Engels, we are reminded that "it is not a question of what this or that proletarian, or even the whole proletariat, at the moment *regards* as its aim. It is a question of *what the proletariat is,* and what in accordance with this *being (Sein),* it will historically be compelled to do" (Marx and Engels 1975: 44 emphasis in original). The state's aim, over many decades, has been to keep that "historical" necessity from the gaze of the working class. In this, the state has been successful. For how much longer, is the question.

What does it all mean for capital, and the state?

The stakes are becoming increasingly high for all concerned. On one side sits the state and capital and on the other an estranged and alienated working class and a shrinking and precariously placed middle class. Each side have different and antagonistic requirements. It is becoming increasingly difficult to paper over these differences. So, what to do? Can the state ever again achieve equilibrium? It is a question that clearly keeps many awake. Keeping things stable is the task of the state. Maintaining a sense of legitimacy, of unity, of order, has been the role of the state since capitalism began its ascendency. It was never easy but is a whole lot more difficult today. Nevertheless, the state ploughs on.

The economic base upon which capitalist society rests is framed by class antagonisms. The working class and its allies have remained largely acquiescent. It has already been shown that the state has acted, over time, to mask and smooth over the most dangerous expressions of class antagonisms. The state acts to defend its and capital's position. As Engels pointed out when commenting on apparent ruling-class accommodation to the needs of the working class, it is for an objective reason. "The fact that all these concessions to justice and philanthropy were nothing else but means to accelerate the concentration of capital into the hands of the few" (Engels 1984: 27). This, in turn, directly relates to the degree that organisations which have traditionally represented the working class, in both a political as well as an economic sense, have become incorporated into the structures of the state. For a class-based society to function in relative harmony, there must be a degree of acceptance that the *status quo* represents the best interests of all. The state recognised from the very earliest days of capitalist rule that force and overt coercion could not be a permanent feature of society. At the same time, the simple fact remains that the ruling class is in a permanent state of struggle, which in turn invites a reaction. The tendency toward "struggle" is less explosive, however, if the capacity for class consciousness is dimmed. "For a class to be ripe for hegemony means that its interests and consciousness enable it to organise the whole of society in accordance with those interests" (Lukacs 1976: 52). Lukacs was specifically writing of the potential for the working class to actively promote its own interests, but it equally describes how the ruling class has managed class relations. This is doubtless the case and it has been a strategy that has been successfully employed for generations. But things are changing in that regard, and new realities confront the state. New ways have to be found if the state is to maintain its grip on things.

Central to the "old ways" of state functioning was to give, and to actively promote, at least an outward appearance of unity. If Engels was correct (and every statistic that appears proves that he was correct) in his assertion that the "main task" was to shift as much wealth as possible into as few hands as possible, then something close to a miracle is in order if capitalism is to keep a lid on things. The ideological fog is slowly thinning. So, what to do? It seems impossible to suggest that the state and capital can or would engage in any reforms of the economic system. It might well offer political reforms, engage with some or many of the protest and identity politics movements, but the core business remains one of economic control and the extraction of the maximum profit from the labour of the working class in every part of the world.

There would appear to be only two possible alternatives for the state. One is to offer concessions, which is most unlikely given all that has been discussed already. The other is to become authoritarian and repressive. This would have a rather short life expectancy as the people have a certain set of expectations and, regardless of the fact that their organisations – political parties of social democracy and the trade unions – have long been co-opted into the service of state, the working class would become rather restive, to say the very least. It is a dilemma and one that seems to be without a satisfactory answer for capitalism or its state.

Two things, seemingly separate and unrelated, appear before us. The first pertains to the state and its move towards authoritarianism. There has been a tendency in the last decade or so to promote fear as a precursor to strengthening laws that ostensibly will protect sovereign rights, borders or national security. Fear, after all, is a great motivator. The endless "war on terror" has been a boon in this respect. Mental health issues, growing anxiety, alienation, the very breakdown of society, throw up behaviours that threaten. Sadly, rather than seeking to resolve any of these background issues, the state and large sections of the media tend to point the finger and demand that we be made safer and more secure. In doing so, we most often hand over rights and freedoms, although there is also a nagging feeling that the exchange is less than fair. There has been a steady erosion of long-held and cherished freedoms. The often ill-defined "other" is brought out to show us all how tenuous things are. Nationalism is fanned and fear grows.

The second is far more subtle. This view of the world sees capitalism as being really much maligned. All it needs is a little tinkering at the edges and it is back in order and something to be admired once more. In recent years there has been an explosion of ideas that seek to do just this. Investors, potential investors, and alarmed and fearful sections of the middle class, for instance, are encouraged to consider what has been labelled "ethical" capitalism. You would have to admit that adding the word ethical to anything gives it a cosy feel. Paul Collier, a former World Bank economist, in *The Future of Capitalism: Facing the New Anxieties*, is one who argues that all can be well, provided that capitalism assumes an ethical position. How an economic system based on profit which can only be derived from the labour of others can at the same time be "ethical" is a dubious proposition.

Another proponent of this more friendly capitalism is Stanley Bergman, the CEO of Henry Schein Health Care. The company is engaged in providing health care products and services. It is regarded as one of the "good guys" in the capitalist marketplace and may well be. He argues that the problem is not with capitalism; the problem is with those capitalists who focus on the present without caring for the future. Capitalism and capitalists cannot be so easily separated. It is a strategy that is hardly novel. Any problem that can be attributed to capitalism becomes the problem of a few "bad apples" and not the system. A rogue banker, a poor decision, a corrupt politician can be blamed, but never the system itself. All can be set to rights.

"Ethical" capitalism is but one more attempt to convince the public and especially sections of the middle class that it will be alright. It's a little hard to be convinced, but the arguments have the capacity to cloud the consciousness of many who cling to the false hope that things can still work out, despite the devastation, despite the despair and in spite of the evidence.

This, however, is but the tip of the iceberg as capitalism, the state and its spokesmen and women work overtime to shore up support for the unsupportable. Titles such as *Conscious Capitalism: liberating the heroic spirit of business* and *The Ethical Capitalist: how to make business work better for society* are being produced to regain confidence. They sit alongside articles like *Three Ways to Reclaim Legitimacy in Global Governance*, or *Making Capitalism Work Better for Workers*, or *Making Capitalism Work for Everyone*, or *12 Top Tips: how governments can find their legitimacy*, etc., etc. The idea of capitalism and of its general "good" is being peddled with incredible intensity. It's a bit like a cross between an old-style revivalist meeting and a pyramid sales scam. Having to re-sell, to re-market the idea of the dominant paradigm to a population that is less interested in buying the product must be disheartening to those ostensibly in charge. It is certainly disquieting to the rest of the world, but there you are. There are no more legitimate cards left to play. All that remains for capitalism and its state is to seek to crush opposition and lumber on for just a little longer. The path ahead for all of us is a precarious and dangerous one. Capitalism has this rather unsavoury habit of going to war in order to breathe life into the system. It also has a nasty propensity towards authoritarianism and fascism and then there is the little problem of a planet that capitalism has very nearly destroyed.

Chapter 6

The planet aflame

As capitalism spirals out of control, it seriously threatens the people and the planet that we share. The world is really aflame. It has become a difficult time to be alive. The problems affect every moment of our conscious lives. They affect relationships between people, between classes and the continued existence of life. We are threatened as a species by the potential of war and the destruction of the planet from climate change. Early Marxists obviously didn't predict the threat to the planet from climate change but were clear in their appreciation of the capacity for capitalism to plunge the word into barbarism. The term is attributed to Engels, but it was Rosa Luxemburg who famously described the choices facing the world in the middle of WWI:

> Either the triumph of imperialism and the collapse of all civilisation as in ancient Rome, depopulation, desolation, degeneration – a great cemetery. Or the victory of socialism, that means the conscious struggle of the international proletariat against imperialism and its method of war (Luxemburg 2008).

Add weapons of mass destruction, nuclear weapons, conventional weaponry such as the infamous "mother of all bombs" with its blast yield of 11 tons of TNT that the US dropped on Afghanistan not that long ago, more as a warning to the world than anything else, and Luxemburg might have been speaking today

Yes, the world is a dangerous place in which to live. Some will say that it has always been so, but there is a confluence of events, economic crises, political upheavals and irresolvable contradictions that make this time in our history a whole lot more dangerous.

War and the threat of war hang in the air. The threat exists because capitalism still lurches on. Nuclear war is no longer an unthinkable prospect, as reports from Washington and the Pentagon show. Sitting alongside this growing threat to us all is the threat of climate change. Why are these two threats being placed side by side? Surely, they are separate things, separate threats and need to be addressed separately. Up to a point this might be the case, but they stem from the same quarter, and are caused by the same economic and political system that is bringing countless millions to a permanent state of fear, alienation and paralysing anxiety. A great fear stalked the earth at the height of the cold war. This had less to do with a fear of "communism" or of the Soviet Union, but from the threat of nuclear annihilation. The fears have been re-ignited but this time from the threat of extinction at the hands of climate change. During the cold war people were discouraged from sheeting home the blame for possible nuclear war to capitalism. Today the people are still being discouraged from facing up to just who the real culprit is. And so, the twin issues of climate and war threaten to drag us down and threaten the barbarity that Rosa Luxemburg so chillingly described.

The militarisation of society

Among the disturbing things that accompany these anxious days of late capitalism is the steady militarisation of civil society. It is an issue that has caught the eye of many in the academic world. Marcus Schulzke points to a growing body of research that shows the divide between military and civilian spheres in society becoming increasingly eroded (2017: 94). A decade earlier, Peter Kaska (2007) was noting a blurring of distinctions between the police and the military and between war and law enforcement. Something was and clearly is going on and it changes things, but not for the better.

There are obvious and outward signs of a militarisation of civil society across states and continents. The government of Britain has been happy to spend 45 million pounds in order to promote a "military ethos" in its schools. The webpage of the German Bundeswehr (the German armed forces) excitedly informed the public that "believe it or not after 60 years waiting for this day...German Armed Forces Day is being celebrated for the first time". The webpage was full of images of children crawling over tanks. In Australia, it is now almost impossible to find a schoolchild who will not tell you, and believe it to be so, that the Gallipoli campaign in 1915 ensured and secured the rights and freedoms that they have been told they enjoy. Just a few years earlier, such a response would have been unthinkable, but the injection of hundreds of millions of dollars to fan the flames of nationalist sentiment is paying dividends. In 2018, French president Macron pushed for the introduction of "national service" for French youth in order to promote a sense of order, civic duty and national unity. Later in that year he issued his call for a European Union army, in order for Europe to better "defend" itself.

These examples are merely indications of how strategic thinking seems to be developing. Police on the streets in most capitalist countries more and more resemble a military force. A random glance around the world is to see remarkable similarities in how the police are becoming militarised. Terror and responses to terrorism are uniformly used to give the green light to legislation that permits military-style equipment, heavy armour and battlefield weaponry.

Canadian police have been described as sometimes looking more like post-apocalyptic military mercenaries than protectors of the peace. Their hardware now includes vehicles that look just a little out of place in a western capitalist city. You know the sort of thing. Armoured vehicles that we see on our news screens rumbling through the streets of Baghdad or Kabul. The same sights are now common across Europe, the US and Australia. Rather than being seen as intimidating, which is what such shows of force are, the heavily-armed military-styled police in Germany is described as offering psychological reassurance to the public. In the United States, the public felt less than reassured. For a brief time, the transfer of military equipment to the police was halted, but it is now business as usual. The Australian government recently enacted legislation that gives the army the right to take control from the police when protests become violent or order is deemed to be endangered. This legislation came into effect with support from all sides of politics.

The police, regardless of country or continent, more and more resemble each other in their approach to maintaining "order". It is not going too far to see this in terms more of "pacification" of the population rather than a visible force enjoying the support of the population. All governments use the same rhetoric when defending the growing militarisation of the police and the state. Heavily-armed and armoured police are on our streets in response to the threat of terror. The show of military muscle is to foster positive feelings of unity in the face of uncertainty. Yes, terrorism has become a threat, but it is interesting to note that its rise coincides with capitalism's deepening crisis. The refugee crisis is a direct response to the military policies of the US and its allies. It is all a little predictable.

Things are certainly predictable, but even so, there are those special moments. Tear gas and pepper spray are very much the "go to" tools as a means of crowd control for just about all of our police forces. It was a big year in 2019 for tear gas and the US-based company Combined Systems Inc., that produces the lion's share of such weaponry. It supplies not only the domestic market but police forces in Egypt, Israel, Tunisia, Chile, Bolivia, Guatemala, Germany, the Netherlands, Argentina, Thailand and Hong Kong, among others. When US-China relations were hitting rock bottom, the US passed a law prohibiting the export of tear gas to Hong Kong. This, of itself, was a remarkable piece of news. US capitalism sold the gas for the Chinese-backed police to use in street protests. These are surely days of wonder. What is even more extraordinary is that Article 1.5 of the Chemical Weapons Convention, which was signed into effect in 1997 and now has 193 nation-state signatories, prohibits tear gas and pepper spray being used in times of war. It's not alright to spray enemy soldiers with tear gas or pepper spray, but it is alright to gas and spray protesters just about anywhere in the world.

Two rather depressing factors come together. First, we see police forces around the world looking and behaving more as a military force, and not unlike an occupation force. Second, we see states actively promoting an acceptance of militarisation in their communities as a means of promoting a sense of unity and national awareness. Running parallel to these two alarming things is the clear evidence that capitalism is in a crisis from which it cannot recover. There is an undeniable integration of global capitalist interests that is far removed from any sense of nation or state. At the same time the nation-state system is working overtime to maintain a sense of purpose. Two competing and contradictory elements are colliding, just as they collided in the lead up to WWI. Then there was a march toward globalisation of capitalist relations. At the same time individual states sought to halt this march and to impose tariffs, trade restrictions and economic nationalist measures to promote their specific interests. The result was the "war to end all wars." Today we see tensions between states growing and governments promoting values that are worrying ones. Are we right to worry?

When the unthinkable becomes strategy

It would be nice to answer the question, "Are we right to worry?" with a loud and confident no. It would be nice to think that those who point accusing fingers are conspiracy theorists. Surely those who control our economic and political systems, those whose interests are the advancement of capitalist profit, would have learned the bitter lessons of the past. Surely there are sober hands at the tiller. We cannot possibly be living in some nightmarish reality that is being considered as a real and viable policy for the future. Yes, there are conspiracy theorists, but things are somehow worse when those who hold the fate of millions in their hands openly speak of new and catastrophic wars.

What, we might ask, is going on? The drive to militarisation is all but universal and it has a most alarming sense of *déjà vu* about it. A little over a century ago, the world plunged into war. The call to nationalism and nationalist symbolism was carefully promoted. The slaughter was all but unimaginable. The conditions that created that war still echo. We see, today, an integrated global economy in contradiction to a powerful nation-state system. We see fears, animosities and distrust between peoples and states rise as those 1914 echoes reverberate.

Latest figures point to a global military budget of 1.8 trillion dollars. The US accounts for nearly half of that figure and is pressuring its allies to constantly increase military spending. The US, in 2014, announced a 10-year upgrade of its nuclear arsenal, at a cost of one trillion dollars. More recently it scrapped the Intermediate Range Nuclear Forces Treaty (INF). In early 2019, the *Guardian* newspaper (Borger 2019) reported that the US has begun making a new, low-yield nuclear warhead for its Trident missiles that arms control advocates warn could lower the threshold for a nuclear conflict. The *Guardian* article quoted Hans Kristensen, the director of the nuclear information project at the Federation of American Scientists, who asked, "to what extent does this signal a new willingness on the part of the US to start using strategic nuclear weapons in a tactical and very limited way early in a potential conflict?" Low-yield nuclear warheads are also referred to as "useable" nuclear weapons.

Allies of the United States have all been increasing military budgets and pledging to reach the "target" of 2 per cent of GDP, an arbitrary sort of figure that will satisfy the needs of national and international "defence". There is a uniformity about all of this. Economies are in dire straits but there are no recessionary fears when it comes to military spending.

There has been a consistent political campaign, a sleight of hand, with the aim of persuading us that spending on weaponry and the military is almost akin to a new industry policy and not a preparation for war. Unfortunately, there is a bipartisanship in this. Militarisation, for our politicians, means jobs and growth and not potential destruction. Many countries are seeing the greatest increase in spending on military hardware since World War II. The list of new warships, fighter aircraft, anti-shipping missiles, or drones, are spoken of in the gentlest and friendliest of terms. They are not offensive weapons but innocuous requirements for national defence and to keep us "safe".

"Increased capacity of weapons systems makes us safe" might sound a little Orwellian, but it pales when compared to a headline in the November/December 2018 issue of *Foreign Affairs* magazine. The magazine devoted the entire issue to the question of nuclear conflict. One article was elegantly titled: "If you Want Peace, Prepare for Nuclear War: a strategy for the new great-power rivalry" (Colby 2018). It would be nice to think that Elbridge Colby was offering us a warning to pull back from some apocalyptic abyss, but that was not his intent. Colby, incidentally, was one of the principal authors of a paper published by the Pentagon earlier in 2018 explaining that the "war on terror" was effectively over and that the US military was recommitting to the concept of great-power competition and confrontation.

Things can sometimes move quickly and dramatically in international relations. The US-inspired trade war of 2018-2019 began pushing the world toward a new cold war. The original cold war was, of course, at least officially, framed by ideology.

Any new versions are less ideological and more economic in nature. Great powers that are guided by capitalist laws rather than political motivations are vying with each other for dominance. The stakes remain high and especially so given the fragility of the global economy and America's place in that global economy. Tensions between the US and both China and Russia are becoming more and more acute. Interestingly, Colby's article appeared just days before the US announced that it would be withdrawing from the INF Treaty that prohibited Washington and Moscow from developing short and medium-range missiles. Increasingly it would appear that the unthinkable is not only being thought but given serious consideration.

The new thinking, as articulated by Colby, acknowledges that the "risks of nuclear brinkmanship may be enormous, but so is the payoff from gaining a nuclear advantage over an opponent." Yes, this is unthinkable, or it ought to be. Nobody with an ounce of sanity or humanity could countenance such a thing and yet respected and respectable position papers, not the ramblings of deranged individuals, but of institutions with responsibility for the future of the planet, are daily contemplating such nightmarish scenarios.

There is a real, if rarely stated, possibility that those nightmare scenarios could become a reality. We need to bear in mind that seemingly rational individuals and institutions are capable of the greatest acts of barbarism to maintain a shell of their capitalist dream. It is not going too far to say that the people who are most at risk from such "leaders" can place no trust in them. There is no semblance of legitimacy. While the world appears to be on the brink of this precipice, there is another crisis of capitalism that endangers us all. Climate change is that most existential of crises that face the planet and the people. As the planet warms, are we really supposed to look to these same "leaders" to save the day?

Climate and the people

The past couple of decades have been marked by two, connected things. The first is the speed with which climate change is being felt. The "debates" as to whether it was real or not are over. The sceptics or deniers exist, but in ever shrinking numbers. The second is the near universal concern that is consuming the thoughts of the vast majority of people. The awareness of this huge contingent of humanity is astonishing. It is an awareness that springs from observing the obvious. Weather, fires, destruction, the images that daily fill our screens, have all served to form a mass-opinion and mass-consciousness. It has also coalesced around a stated and unstated demand that something must be done.

Those that would seek to deny this existential crisis are becoming fewer and fewer. The old cries, that "the science is divided", are seldom heard anymore. However, while there is near uniformity of will among the people, little is being done of any real substance. The UN World Meteorological Organization (WMO) Secretary-General Petteri Taalas, citing the WMO's annual report, stated that "greenhouse gas concentrations are once again at record levels and if the current trend continues, we may see temperature increases of 3-5 degrees C by the end of the century" (WMO 2019). The teenage activist Greta Thunberg, speaking at the 2019 COP 25 conference, drew attention to the inaction on the part of both politicians and CEOs. All of this raises serious questions. Why is nothing significant being done? How can those being held to account by Thunberg and so many others, go on doing so little, and why are the people, so justly angry, unable to make these same people respond?

These three questions are all part of the same overarching problem upon which this discussion has been based and yet there is an almost qualitative difference to this issue. The people have seldom, if ever, been so aware, so united, so fearful of the future, than they are today. It is an issue that unites or appears to unite people like no other and yet those, purportedly, acting in our interests seem incapable or unwilling to act. What makes things even more interesting is that those same politicians that Thunberg castigates invariably acknowledge that there is a problem. The motivations and dilemmas of the representatives of the state are important and deserve special consideration, but first we need to focus on how the people most affected by all of this have developed the level of consciousness that now appears to exist.

Life has been the great teacher in this respect. Just a couple of decades ago, there was still a degree of scepticism. The loudest voices still belonged to the state and its various representatives. Those who spoke out against this and in support of an ever-growing body of scientific evidence were able, to an extent, to be sidelined. Simplistic and ineffectual actions were advocated. Switching to better lightbulbs, observing "earth hour" actions and turning off the lights massaged the consciences of some but were never going to win the support of the broad mass of society. The evidence of the weather and the dislocated seasons and the simple, word-of-mouth logical discourse that everyone could engage with slowly and then in a cascading fashion won the support of the majority. It was a case of making an idea accessible.

As a consequence of the obvious evidence and the quiet neighbour-to-neighbour exchange of views, the percentages of people across the world who recognise that change must happen is astonishingly high and astonishingly similar. Two-thirds of opinion poll respondents in the UK, US and Australia have called for climate action. The figures are higher in Canada and Germany. It is an issue that unites rather than divides communities. Political theorists might well take note of all this. Responses to climate change and the calls for climate action are political issues. How political forces react to the demands being made by the people become significant. Of equal significance is how the political forces demand that climate change is both developed and focused on by the people on the ground.

This is not by any means endorsement for a people's movement devoid of theory or of leadership. The road to hell, after all, is paved with good intentions. However, armed pretty much only with an awareness that things are wrong and that something must be done, millions have been mobilised. Those who sought to "arm" the nascent movement with a theoretical base have achieved little, except, of course, a degree of confusion. This is especially the case when most theories and theorists still baulk at the final hurdle of laying blame at capitalism's feet.

There are many theories surrounding environmental issues. Despite what ought to be an obvious truth – that the environment has been and is being destroyed by capitalism – much of environmental theory has sought to accommodate the requirements of this movement to capitalism. In the 1970s, "ecophilosophy" emerged in the face of growing environmental awareness. Arne Naes (1973) advanced the concept of "ecophilosophy" as an expression of "deep ecology". He argued that both exploiter and exploited are unable to achieve "self-realisation" and that therefore an "anti-class" posture is required to achieve an ecological egalitarianism (Naes 1973: 96-97). It was a conception that separated class and people and ultimately failed to challenge capitalism as the cause of environmental degradation. It is not a good idea and nor is it appropriate to portray the great mass of people as being in any way the cause of the problems facing the environment. Rather, the people are the victims of destructive capitalist processes. In other words, capitalism, not the people, are the guilty parties. Capitalism has brought the planet to the brink. It is not the people that are driven to return increasing profits, or who must out-perform rivals, find bigger markets and newer ways of extracting resources. Challenges to capitalism from such an "ecophilosophy" are unlikely, despite the claim that "with the decline of socialism, environmentalism becomes the major vantage point of opposition to business-as-usual" (Hay 2002: 341).

The battle of ideology

Theories of how best to approach and tackle this crisis tend to reflect the thinking of the broader society. It could not be otherwise. The left, as has been shown, is in disarray. There is a multiplicity of left, socialist and Marxist positions on just about every aspect of society. To imagine that there would be some universal confluence of ideas around combatting climate change is fanciful. This is not to suggest that those seeking a way forward are not operating from deeply held beliefs, based on interpretations of how best to reorganise society. But good intentions do not always suffice. Prominent among the ideological perspectives that confront the potential climate change activists are those of "green socialism" or "eco-socialism", "green anarchism" and the green new deal movement. These propositions deserve to be considered.

Green or eco-socialism takes as its starting point that an expanding capitalism is the cause of the problem. So far so good. It argues for the "dismantling" of capitalism and for common ownership. However, what is immediately disturbing is in its quite explicit appeal to "middle class environmentalists" and to "working class socialists". It would appear that in their thinking there is a divide between the two and that they are somehow mutually exclusive sub-sets of society. The eco-socialist movement was launched in the US in 2013 at a conference that proclaimed that a big step forward had been taken in creating an anti-capitalist wing of the environmental movement. The aims of such a movement may be laudable; to oppose capitalist expansion. There is more than a touch of utopianism about it all when it describes setting up a world people's trade organisation that will democratise and improve world trade. Such a fundamental change in the order of things is difficult to imagine without there being a serious backlash from the capitalism that is being opposed. We end up with a bit of Marx, a bit of utopian thought, a bit of hope, a bit of this and a bit of that.

For some activists even this still bears the hallmarks of an authoritarian, hierarchical structure. Enter green anarchism. Green anarchists, like the green socialists, are seeking to develop an anti-capitalist agenda. Theirs is a little broader. Green anarchists are concerned not only with the fate of human society, but with what they describe as the "non-human world" as well. This is not merely a call to protect animals, but a move to abolish all forms of hierarchy. Corin Bruce (2019) argues that "it is not merely humans that are the victims of state, capitalist, and – more generally – hierarchical destruction: the common victims of this complex of domination are ultimately all forms of life on Earth" (Bruce 2014). The approach of the anarchists may not resonate with all, but it has won a sizeable constituency.

Extinction Rebellion (ER) captured the headlines in 2019. It represents an attempt to merge theory and practice. While it would be wrong to align this group too closely with the green anarchists, there are some similarities. What is significant about ER is their loose organisational structures and their overarching "three" demands. In abbreviated form these are: that government tell the truth and declare a state of emergency, that government act to halt biodiversity loss and that government create and be led by a citizens' assembly. ER has certainly built a strong constituency, particularly amongst the youth, but it is interesting that it appeals directly to "government" rather than pointing the finger at capitalism that caused the crisis in the first place.

Herein lie some really significant issues and problems for any movement that would challenge the *status quo*. It also brings us to what has been presented as the movement for a "Green New Deal". The GND movement has won some very illustrious supporters. Numbers of political figures in the US, including Al Gore and Joe Biden, have lent their support to this campaign that sets itself the task of addressing climate change and economic inequality, both of which certainly need addressing. It has also won the support of writers and advocates. Naomi Klein, for example, in her *On Fire: The Burning Case for a Green New Deal* (2019), goes to some lengths to point out the problems and to a degree lays blame at the feet of the capitalist system. She goes so far as to state that "we have not done the things that are necessary to lower emissions because those things fundamentally conflict with deregulated capitalism" (2019: 18). However, the book ends up seeking ways to make capitalism work better. Such calls have been made in all spheres of endeavour ever since capitalism emerged as the dominant system but to little or no effect.

The US Congress has before it a Green New Deal Resolution (H. Res 109 2019) which has generated much support. It calls for the US to become the international leader on climate action and for investments to spur economic development in regional economies. What it explicitly does not do is issue a call for an international degree of cooperation nor restrict the activities of energy corporations. The central plank of the "deal" is to allocate funds to community grants and public banks who will work with US energy monopolies. Public money, it would appear, is to be siphoned into the coffers of these monopolies that are largely responsible for so much of the crisis in the first place.

The fact remains that for the vast majority of people who daily worry about climate change, who take part in protest actions, who talk to others, the ideological issues are of no special relevance. They simply want something to be done. The problem is, however, that little is being done. This is due in part to a degree of intransigence from those who created the problem in the first place and by the confusion that stems from there being either no leadership or poor leadership of this movement. Without a clear idea of where you are going and how you expect to arrive, then nothing can be really achieved that will resolve this or any other issue.

Capitalism, one might reasonably assume, must be as aware and as fearful of the future as anybody holding a placard in any demonstration anywhere in the world. After all, we either all have a future or none of us do.

Capitalism and climate

How then does capitalism and its state regard this most existential of problems? Well, to begin with, we need to remember that capitalism, while controlling the state, does not necessarily always speak with one voice. The media will supply many examples of capitalist enterprises, individual capitalists and the like who are making all the right noises and being seen to be doing the right thing. What is important is not that sections of capital might have competing aims and strategies (which is doubtless the case) but to step back a little and view the picture in its entirety. Earlier, reference was made to the working class and its degree of class awareness or class consciousness. Marx and Engels were quoted. It is well to repeat that quote but, in this reading, simply replace proletarian with capitalist and capitalism. "It is not a question of what this or that proletarian, or even the whole proletariat, at the moment *regards* as its aim. It is a question of *what the proletariat is*, and what in accordance with this *being (Sein)*, it will historically be compelled to do" (Marx and Engels 1975: 44 emphasis in original).

The problem that the world faces is a problem of capitalism. At the top sit the great polluters, the great emitters. Flowing down from them comes the entire structure of a contradiction-ridden society. The drive to insane levels of consumption in the name of maintaining profits, the seeming inability to handle the waste and detritus of capitalist society, and the anxiety people feel when they see the planet swamped with rubbish, and burning, is all the problem, the fault of the entire capitalist system and not the efforts of a rogue group of capitalists.

It needs to be borne in mind that just 100 capitalist corporations in the world account for 71 per cent of total carbon emissions. It needs also to be borne in mind that these corporations are only notionally linked to any nation-state. Capital has long ago broken the fetters of national boundaries. At the same time individual nation-states exist in a perpetual state of rivalry, each seeking the greatest advantage in an insane game of international politics and economics. These two elements of capitalist relations, the great contradiction between globalised capitalism and the nation-state, indicate that the way forward for significant and lasting solutions to climate change is fraught with difficulty.

But surely states and national governments are duty-bound to ensure that something meaningful is done, not only to allay fears but to ensure survival? That is a logical argument and efforts are being made at governmental and state level. However, what also needs to be remembered is that states represent geographic areas while capital is less encumbered. Fingers are pointed at nation-states that are doing little and praise is given to states that are doing well. Some even suggest that capitalism can and must reorganise itself to solve the problem. All of this needs a very brief examination.

There are states that appear recalcitrant. This is no secret. There are others that enjoy a good reputation. These countries are being seen to reduce their emissions and so why can't the rest? The fact is that there are nearly 200 nation-states, and all are seeking to some degree to gain comparative advantages in trade and economic relationships. A country may well eliminate energy production that uses fossil fuels, while still buying energy from polluting states. It is just one small example. Capitalist corporations, too, will be sometimes seen to be doing the right thing, or at least in relation to their "home-territory", while going about business as usual in any number of developing states.

The majority of the biggest polluting corporations are, significantly, based in the US, but Japan, Germany, the UK, Australia, the Netherlands among others are also in the "A" list of global emitters. They might not be laying waste to home soil, but this counts for little. There are also those like Warren Buffett who stated in a letter to share-holders that "inaction now is foolhardy" (Cushman 2016). It read well but his company, Berkshire Hathaway, still sits in fourth place among global corporations in the greenhouse rankings and thirteenth in toxic air ratings and nothing appears to be happening in the Buffett empire except that his wealth has grown since his 2016 warning. What is particularly disturbing is that men such as Buffett know what is happening and know what to do. They make all the right noises but the quest for profit ultimately overrides all else.

And then in the face of what would seem to be the absolutely indefensible, there are those apostles of capitalism that beaver away producing books, articles and lecture series that seek to convince us that capitalism is the best chance we all have to resolve the problems of climate change. Now this might sound absurd but with each new and deeper crisis in the capitalist economy, the same, or at least similar, voices look for capitalism to save the day. Andrew McAfee (2019), of MIT, has captured the imagination of many in his new book, *More From Less: the surprising story of how we learned to prosper using fewer resources and what happens next*. It seeks to invoke the memory of a capitalism, now long passed, that was both progressive and forward thinking. There is an obvious problem here. With each passing year global emissions rise, ocean pollution gets worse, ice-caps melt and temperatures rise. McAfee's claims that more capitalism and more innovative capitalism is and will do the trick is simply absurd.

This same intelligent, problem-solving capitalism is beginning to feel the economic cost of the crisis. It is estimated that global stock markets might lose as much as $2 trillion in value over the next few years. The cost won't be getting any smaller as the years go by. However, the problem is able to be solved and capitalism knows this as well as anybody else. While still talking in terms of dollars and cents, it is estimated that the total and complete cost of cleaning up the mess and repairing the planet would cost $50 trillion by 2050 (Klebnikov 2019). Governments, so much a part of the capitalist system, are unlikely to be funding this, and it is extremely unlikely that individual capitalist corporations will be opening up their wallets any time soon. Fifty trillion dollars is, after all, a lot of money. It's a figure that is difficult to imagine. A little earlier in the chapter the annual global military budget was given as being $1.8 trillion. It is ludicrous to suggest, but if $50 trillion is to be found by 2050, then it is still less than the outlay for weaponry over the same period. There is also the fact that there is $360 trillion in accumulated wealth on the planet at the moment. So, if governments won't find the funds and capitalism won't cooperate, then what are we to do?

The people live in separate nation-states. This is an inescapable fact of life. They also increasingly live in a globalised world. The global population is actively discouraged from seeing itself as anything but citizens of separate states, and states that are increasingly in competition, one with another. The governments of these competing nation-states invariably "say" the right things but fall far short of what is required. Just as socialism cannot be built in a single country but is an international task, neither can climate change be halted and reversed in a single country. This is not to surrender. What can be done, must be done at every stage. It can and must be countered. Whatever action that can be taken at a state level needs to be taken but for a satisfactory end-result, there must be a global commitment. It must be a global affair and one not encumbered by capitalism.

The century is now 2 decades old. As the clocks marked the new millennium, there were many doomsayers and apocalyptic "visionaries" who foretold the end of the world. It didn't end, but capitalism appears to be hell-bent on bringing that apocalyptic vision to reality. Billions of people are engaged in a daily struggle for survival. In the "affluent" west there is fear, anxiety, alienation and uncertainty. Nation-states are engaging in dangerous games of brinkmanship. The century has experienced constant war and a militarisation of society. The most powerful state on the planet, the US, is producing new weapons, both nuclear and what are laughingly called "conventional", and openly speaks of "useable" nuclear weapons. Other global powers follow suit in a revival of cold war thinking. The only difference is that this time around the cold war is being driven, as previously stated, not by ideology but by economic crisis. The planet smoulders and burns as an environmental catastrophe unfolds.

According to Greek mythology, Pandora opened the "box" and allowed all of the evils to escape. Only hope remained. Hope may "spring eternal" but we need more than hope to fix up the mess that capitalism has given us. Capitalism is incapable of resolving the problems of its creation. No single nation-state can resolve the problems. No amount of anguish or occupying the streets will resolve the problems. This might sound like words of despair. Far from it. Something has to be done and something can be done to sort things out and get us all out of that cauldron of anxiety.

Chapter 7

What is to be done?

Something has to be done. Just what and how are huge questions. There is an underlying cause of the problems that we all face, and that cause has been identified. That, after all, should not be all that difficult, although there appears to be precious little by way of meaningful challenge to the cause of our woes. Knowing that something is wrong is the first step in resolving the problem. The second is to identify the source of the problem, but when the problem is the entire economic and political structures that have framed our lives for generations, the third and final step, of working out what is to be done, becomes a whole lot more difficult.

It is easy, but never good enough, to simply say these are all problems of capitalism and they can only be solved by doing away with capitalism and replacing it with socialism, even if it is the truth. The radical left media have, for decade upon decade, ended articles with a quick rounding off of the argument saying, "only with the establishment of a socialist government will this (insert any issue) be resolved". It has always been true but so often leaves the reader just a little dissatisfied. It does display a sense of optimism, but something is missing. Generations of "sober" socialists have warned against being falsely or unrealistically optimistic. "The revolution is not about to happen any time soon. We must remain patient." This has doubtless been the truth, but an air of fatalism creeps in, which is just one step ahead of a sense of demoralisation. However, as Marx and Engels so succinctly put it, "philosophers have only interpreted the world, in various ways; the point is to change it" (Marx and Engels 1964: 647).

If the point is to change the world, then how to go about

doing it is important. That is the business of the following pages. We know what we don't want – capitalism and the pain that it is inflicting on humanity and the planet. We know that there is a better way, a better future and a future that could work.

Marxism offers a guide, not in the sense of a self-help guide, but as a road-map out of the morass that is capitalism. It has never been, and nor should it be in any way, a prescriptive thing. But, by the same token, there are some pointers on this map that we can all accept. For instance, there is a need for political leadership, and a theory that can arm the people. How things pan out is dependent on unforeseeable issues and complications. However, Marxism does still offer that guide. An immediate question arises. If this is the case, then why has it not been a bit more successful? After all Marxism has been around for a good while. Didn't it simply miss the boat and its moment in time? The question needs an answer. Capitalism has survived, not because of any intrinsic strengths but, to a large extent, because Marxism and Marxist organisations have not been able to offer a serious challenge. There are a range of reasons why this has been the case. They require consideration. And so, we need to have a brief look at what Marxism is, what it is for and how it got itself into the mess that it did.

Despite its historical problems, Marxism offers the best option, the only option to confront and defeat capitalist rule. This can only be achieved through political organisation and through re-invigorating the concept of class struggle. This is happening, to some degree, of itself. The working class around the world is engaging in massive struggles against the state and capital. These struggles are invariably being defeated, or more accurately, the forces of the state are currently able to maintain the upper hand, sometimes by real force and more often by thinly veiled threats of force. Defeats and set-backs are a consequence of a failure to integrate a theory that Marxism offers with a practice that can offer more than just hope.

Marxism offers that hope, but not the hope that remained in Pandora's box and not the hope that somehow, somewhere, sometime, someone will make things better or that things might return to how they appeared to be in a past.

What is Marxism and what is it for?

Critics of Marxism are quick to point out that the theory has not had a terribly good track record. Not only do they point out this obvious fact but point it out with an almost unseemly glee. This is, of itself, interesting. Marxism is also routinely written off by these same anti-Marxists as being irrelevant, somehow ahistorical and dead. If this were true, then why do the critics so willingly continue to wage war? The criticisms are unavoidable and need to be seriously addressed. Capitalism has been in crisis for the past century and, yet, here we are talking about a Marxist challenge that never seems to get any closer. This needs to be acknowledged, and problems addressed and resolved, if the future is not to be one of barbarism.

The first thing that needs to be reinforced is that Marxism is all about class. It is a theory based on the knowledge that capitalism is a class-based economic and political structure and can only exist if there is exploitation of class by class, and, for preference, a strong dose of subservience on the part of the exploited. Today the global working class stands at more than 3.5 billion and for the first time in history, the working class constitutes pretty much the majority of the world's population. Marxism's task is to harness this vast potential for change and to provide the leadership required to effect change.

It would be reasonable to assume that this simple fact, the weight of numbers and the global nature of the working class would be a unifying thing for Marxists, but no, this is not the case. Marxism is decidedly dis-united, and class is one of the issues that serves the cause of disunity. The problem has been a long time in the making. The incapacity of the Marxist left to challenge capitalism essentially has its genesis in the rise of Stalinism. Marxist theorists at the time of Stalin's rise in the period following the Russian Revolution were faced with some big choices. They could, of course, simply accommodate themselves to Stalin. This was the course chosen by the majority of activist Marxists, within the communist parties, although it was not always as simple as making a well-informed choice. An alternative was to maintain what might be called a classical Marxist approach, closely aligned to the theories of Marx and Engels, as well as Lenin, Trotsky, Luxemburg and others. It was an approach that sought to maintain a sense of theory and practice and was constantly attacked, often to the point of death, as was the case with Trotsky. The third option was to seek a way to "rescue" the theory by adapting it to the new conditions that Stalinism created. To be fair, the rescuers were acting in good faith, but each mission that was launched to save Marxism took the theory another step away from the core business of changing the world. Piece by piece, bits were metaphorically shaved off the central planks of Marxism. We don't need to delve too deeply into the sorry history of Marxist theory in the past century. It was a time of crisis within the Marxist movement, a movement whose task it was to offer ideological leadership to counter capitalism. The conflict that engulfed Marxism and continues to do so was reflected in differences in method. Neither the 1917 Russian Revolution, World War I nor the Depression led to capitalist collapse. Consequently, many Marxist theorists began to question the Marxist approach, regarding it as insufficient to address new realities that arose from what appeared to be failures in theory and practice. Neo-Marxists sought, among other things, to replace the class essence of Marxist method with one that focused on social conflicts. The essential Marxist proposition of class as the determining feature of societal and economic development and therefore a pivot around which capitalist development revolves was similarly called into

Then there are the voices who sing virtual hymns of praise for the infallible system. Robert Gilpin enthusiastically spoke of a new age of global capitalism. "Americans, other citizens of the industrialized world, and many people in other parts of the international economy have entered what the financial expert and economic commentator Hale has called 'The Second Great Age of Global Capitalism'" (2000: 15). Unfortunately, or possibly fortunately, such extravagant claims rapidly become dated and take on an even more extravagant tone. The Global Financial Crisis, as an expression of the deepening crisis in capitalism, the retreat into economic nationalism, the clearly irresolvable contradictions between globalised capitalism and the nation-state all serve to make such exaltation laughable. Gilpin (2000: 51) further argued that economic efficiency and the ambitions of dominant nation-states will determine the future power and prosperity of global capitalism. Those same "ambitions" might well see the world engulfed in war, but if he is correct, then Marxism has no future and therefore no purpose. On the other hand, Marxism has not been disproven. On the contrary, the very problems within capitalism attest to the validity of Marxism. Marxist analysis, however acute and accurate it might be, has not led to change. Is Marxism to simply be a useful tool to analyse that which can be observed, or a vehicle by which to bring about change? In answering this question, we need to linger a while in Marxist theory.

Marx (1964: 31-32) built his method of analysis on the premise that the first historically significant moment for human development was the production of the economic means to satisfy material requirements and needs. Obviously, this means that there could be no advance in civilisation without advances in material production, but equally that those advances determine the nature of civilisation. In this case it means the development of relationships are framed by the class nature of society.

Marxist theory, therefore, rests on the notion that economic factors largely determine social and political actions and reactions. For some this becomes a problem. John Gray, while rejecting what he considers to be Marxism's failed attempt at social engineering, is still forced to accept that "in market societies. . .not only is economic activity distinct from the rest of social life, but it conditions, and sometimes dominates, the whole of society" (2002: 12). "Marxists" and those claiming a heritage that springs from Marxism, are absolutely free to develop theories, but all too often what we end up with is a tangled web of convolution and confusion.

The simple fact is that the future of Marxism and the question of what Marxism is for is intimately connected with economic issues and with Marx's own emphasis on economics. For many critics of Marx, both non-Marxist and from within the broad Marxist milieu, the issue of Marx's "economism" becomes the nub of Marxism's "problems" and therefore an obstacle to a "future" for Marxism. Andrew Gamble's simple defence is more than apt, arguing that:

> Marxism in the end has to stand by the claim that the economic power which accrues to the class which controls productive assets is a crucial determinant of the manner in which political, cultural and ideological power are exercised. Many kinds of sophisticated concepts can be deployed to understand the intricacies of the relationship, but in the end if the primacy of the economic is lost, then Marxism loses its distinctiveness and its value in social theory (1999: 143).

Much of the ongoing crisis within Marxism stems from a perceived need to distance Marxism from its "economism" and its "determinism". Western Marxism and its variations have, for decades, sought to reconstruct Marxist theory. This has been at the expense of core Marxist considerations of the centrality of economics. In its place has grown a misplaced acceptance that societal and political issues inform economic questions. Despite this, the crisis of capitalism has continued to indicate that economic issues do, indeed, play a central role in determining social and political outcomes. Marxism offers a theory and an analytical framework from which to build resistance to capitalism. This resistance must necessarily address the primacy of economic questions. This, in Marxist theory, boils down to a core assumption. This is the issue of base and superstructure. The economic structures of society and capitalism constitute the base. Social and political activities and the institutions of the state (the superstructure) rest on this economic base. Fundamental change can only be effected by changing the base. If the point of Marxism is to change the world then the economic structures of that world must be addressed, understood and changed.

Change, according to Marxist theory, takes place within the context of class conflict. The working class and its allies assume an historical role. What is meant by this is that any successful campaign against capitalist rule can only be achieved if the working class has the ability to promote a political vision that will empower it. Such a vision, in turn, can only be successful if there is a leadership that is independent from the state and its institutions and enjoys the support of the working class. This is where things begin to assume a sense of urgency in the twenty-first century, as the working class, its allies and the entire planet are ever more immediately threatened by capitalism's continued existence. Michael Lebowitz, in an interview on the relevance of Marx in the twenty-first century, remarked:

> I think that there is absolutely no question that Marxism enables us to understand the nature of the capitalist crisis today. For non-Marxists, everything is an accident or the result of bad decisions. They are not able to distinguish between causes and effects and often see symptoms as the source of problems. In contrast, Marxism permits us

to consider capitalism as a whole and to understand the underlying factors which characterize not only its crises but also its periods of uninterrupted expansion.

However, I think it is an error to think that Marxism can solve the crisis. Marxism is a theory – it is a way to understand. Ultimately, the only way to end capitalist crises is to end capitalism. And that requires more than a theory; it requires a commitment and determination to put an end to this perverse economic system (2013).

If Marxism is no more than a theory and a guide to understanding how the world turns, then it remains and must remain incapable of effecting change. Marxism has historically sought to present a theoretical response to capitalism while simultaneously promoting a practice that would enable an ideologically armed working class to assume the status of ruling class. Such has been the "theory" of Marxism. The "practice" has often been quite a different matter. Isaac Deutscher (1973: 18) described a rift between theory and practice that divided classical Marxism from Western Marxism and the New Left. It was a reminder of two of Marxism's more famous aphorisms – that without revolutionary theory there can be no revolutionary movement and that practice without theory is blind and that theory without practice is sterile.

In much the same sense that Robert Cox (1981: 128) argues that theory is always for someone and for some purpose, then so too is Marxism for a particular purpose. That purpose is to promote a theory and practice that will equip the working class to confront and combat capitalism. Central to this purpose is Marxism's capacity to respond to, address and provide answers to the questions that capitalism, in the twenty-first century, raises. Marxism, then, has relevance, it has purpose and it has a future. It exists to counter capitalism in an age of capitalist crisis. But how can this be achieved?

A brighter future

Classical Marxist literature, or rather the words of those early Marxists – Marx, Engels, Lenin, Trotsky, Luxemburg and the rest – share a pithy, simple and accessible style. Perhaps it was because they were writing for a specific audience and knew their audience well. They were writing for workers and they had the ability to quickly "cut to the chase". It is an observation worth contemplating when thinking about organisational structures for the future.

To secure that future means overcoming the "crisis of leadership" that Trotsky referred to and that so clearly exists. The working class is the class that can bring about fundamental change, but it requires an awareness, a consciousness of its power and a conscious leadership, both from within the class and from its allies. It requires a resolute guide to action. The most obvious form of such leadership is one based in Marxist theory and practice. This is best represented in that special form of political organisation, the Marxist political party. If capitalism is to be confronted, then there needs to be a way of preparing for and organising that confrontation.

There has been no shortage of historical moments that might have led to change and challenge, and yet capitalism remains obviously in charge. The failures of the working-class movement can be attributed, as Trotsky (1974) so forcefully did, to a failure of leadership of the working class and, it must be admitted, there have been many failures. Some have been the result of poor leadership and some can be directly linked to the impact of Stalinism. The German revolution, the Chinese revolution of 1925-1927, the British General Strike of 1926, the Spanish Civil War were all moments that were lost. Stalinism remains, undoubtedly, the common denominator. Other "lost" moments can be attributed to a lack of leadership, the spontaneity of events and a lack of programme. Many of these spring from a denial of the need of political leadership which again is a reflection of the influence of Stalinism on the working-class movement and of a mistrust of Marxist politics that grew in the wake of the Stalinisation of Marxism.

The realities that confront the world and the global working class in the twenty-first century, however, make it necessary to rethink, to abandon the past and to reconsider Marxism as a path to a better future. There is a need of a political movement that has consistent and independent leadership. The working class has been caught in the web of state-sponsored nationalist sentiment, promoting the view that "we" have aims and aspirations in common despite the divisions that class-rule demands, promoting the belief that global problems can be resolved nationally, or even locally, and that the institutions of the state can miraculously resolve all problems. The events of 2019 and into 2020 would indicate that this web is beginning to unravel.

A socialist consciousness, a class consciousness, is fundamental to breaking free from that web. Such a consciousness can grow in the working class, but significantly from forces working alongside the working class, developing the theory that will inform practice. This can be a long and painstaking process. Patience is a virtue but the times demand that something be done. However, that something cannot in any way rely on spontaneous actions. We have seen enough to have learned that lesson. Nor can it rely on the siren call of identity politics. The political expression that is demanded can only be based on an internationalist perspective and have nothing to do with the promotion of nationalist responses to what are global questions.

Marxists who take their cue from the ideas of classical Marxism are clear in what is required from a political organisation and how it needs to address the problems at hand. Marx and Engels (1977: 49) first outlined what they believed to be the core elements, the core business of such an organisation. For them, and subsequent classical Marxists, the essence of a communist organisation is that it operates in the interests of the working class, regardless of nationality and in the direct interests of the movement as a whole. For them the challenge to capitalism was to come through a political party structure and that this party could only be organised at the global level. This becomes even more relevant today as capitalism has assumed an intensely global character. The significance of Marxism in this period lies in its insistence upon its organisational capacity, its independence, its internationalism, its analytical abilities and a capacity to merge theory with practice.

So, what does this party look like? If we know what we want, why not just get on with the job? It is always a big temptation to set out a series of pre-conditions, to wave wands, to be dogmatic, to be prescriptive about things. What form of political organisation it takes is necessarily dependent upon the objective conditions that exist, but even so, some things stand out. What is clear is that the essential formation of any such political organisation cannot be limited by national boundaries and nor could it hope to exist under the "patronage" of the state that it ultimately would seek to challenge and replace. John Rees describes a situation whereby:

> a revolutionary organization remains the indispensable tool...Without the struggle to build such an organization, the danger remains that the dialectic of capitalist development will remain...but if the struggle to build such an organization is successful, we have a chance – not more, not less – to make the leap from the realm of necessity to the realm of freedom (1998: 301-302).

There is something of a "call to arms" about all this and yes it is a call to arms. Why? Because the option of ignoring things, of hoping for the best, of trusting to the better nature of capitalism or individual capitalists will only end disastrously. Capitalism has developed to the point at which there is nowhere to go. We are on the edge of a dangerous abyss. If we are not to be pushed into that abyss, then change must happen. This is what Marxism, and a political expression of Marxism, is all about and why, despite a century of crisis, the future can be bright.

And so...to business

A good many people are calling for something better than the fear and anxiety that goes with life under late capitalism. According to opinion polls, there are millions prepared to consider socialism in a favourable light. While there are a range of opinions as to just what socialism means, the preparedness to simply utter the word by so many is of itself important and a step forward. If socialism is a destination worth arriving at, then how to get there? The state is not going to simply hand over the reins of power because a majority of those surveyed in an opinion poll say that socialism is a good idea. The tiny band of capitalist "masters of the universe" are unlikely to slip away into retirement. We have all heard the chants at rallies and protests: "what do we want (insert demand), when do we want it – now" but no matter how loud the chant, or how many times it is repeated, capitalism is not about to surrender its grip on power. This is where Marxist theory and practice becomes relevant and required.

Well, you might expect a Marxist to say that. The non-Marxist, the anti-Marxist might dismiss this as delusional. They are free to do so. A leap of faith is not required but it would be well to remember that things are wildly out of control and neither capitalism nor its state is willing or capable of offering any lifelines. It also needs to be borne in mind that more and more people are consciously seeking an alternative, seeking something better. Achieving that requires a lot of work. It is work that begins in the often-thin atmosphere of theory and moves to the more concrete world of practice.

There are probably thousands of books devoted to various aspects of Marxist theory. Marx and Engels' *Collected Works* adds up to 50 volumes on their own, but one slim book stands out. A remarkable event occurred in 1848. A little book, barely 100 pages in length, was published. It was Marx and Engels' *Manifesto of the Communist Party*. It has rarely been out of print. Millions of copies have been produced in all languages spoken on the planet. It has influenced and continues to influence people around the world. It speaks in a language and style that is accessible, and its message has remained relevant across the decades. When *Penguin* brought out its *Little Black Classics*, featuring 80 classic titles, the *Manifesto* was by far its best seller. Why? The answer is in the message that the book, and Marxism, delivers. It bodes well for the future, or at least it ought to.

Understanding Marx and the message of Marxism is not difficult. The difficulties only began to present themselves when contemporary Marxist theorists set to work to "rescue" Marxism, to make it "relevant", to adapt it to fit new realities, and in so doing, clouded the language and message in a miasma of confusion. Theory was layered over theory until the original message was all but lost. The seeker of wisdom and truth today must pick their way through a minefield of "ideas" that seem, and rightly so, more and more distant from the ideas of the early classical Marxists. Which current of Marxism, which school, which thread is to be followed? Is it to be Western, or libertarian, or structural or cultural, or analytical Marxism? Perhaps it might be neo-Marxism, or Marxist Humanism, or Marxist Feminism or even post-Marxist Marxism. The analysis of classical Marxists is devalued by these schools of thought. Each strand becomes more and more obtuse, less readable and, ultimately, just confusing. Things no longer make sense. The more one reads, the less sense it all makes. Then, seemingly credible voices explain that Marxism is no longer relevant, that the working-class is no longer relevant and that the ideas that sprang so clearly from the pages of the *Manifesto* are no more than the noble thoughts of a long dead philosopher and economist. Theory and theorists become further removed from practice, but then practice, too, has suffered from the same fog of confusion.

The practice of Marxism has come to reflect this disconnected theory. It would seem logical that as the crisis of capitalism becomes ever more obvious, then organised political expressions of Marxism would strengthen. This has not happened, although there remain numerous organisations claiming to be Marxist, and there are reasons why this has been the case. It is no easy thing to live and work in a world that is so intensely "bourgeois" in its thinking. To be a socialist, a Marxist, to not just want something better, but to act to achieve that outcome, is to be forever swimming against the tide. It has been something with which Marxists have had to contend for a very long time and has contributed to the ongoing crisis within Marxism. It has always been difficult to maintain an intellectual framework that could withstand bourgeois ideology. Trotsky wrote of this dilemma in describing how many, "when thrown against great events... are easily lost and relapse again into petty-bourgeois ways of thinking" (1971: 59). This, and the crisis in Marxist thought and practice, has bedevilled the movement for a century and has led to confusion within political organisations. How then to maintain equilibrium and a sense of optimism? It can and must be done. How can we move forward in these times of intense anxiety for the people, and times of intense crisis for capitalism?

Regardless of a distorted theory that effectively diminished the prospect of successful political practice, the future lies in Marxist theory and practice; in political organisation. The times demand that this be so. Capitalism doesn't work. We know that. Socialism offers an alternative. We know that. We also know that there are any number of political parties trying to sell one version or another of the socialist vision.

Yes, there are many left parties and tendencies vying for

attention, but while socialists might call for equality, not all ideas are equal. It is an unfortunate fact of life and flows from the distortions in theory and practice that have so marred Marxism's development. Even so, it is in the form of political organisation and Marxist theory that hope can become reality. A Marxist political party that can challenge capital needs to be marked by certain features. These include a clear recognition that:

- Capitalism can only survive by exploiting the working class. The interests of the working class and those of the ruling class are fundamentally opposed. Class, therefore, is important.
- Capitalism can only be defeated by an economic and political struggle by the working class with a political and theoretical leadership that comes from Marxism. Political campaigns that are based on race, ethnicity, gender, sexuality or any variant of identity politics will never and can never challenge the rule of capital. No amount of reform will threaten capitalist rule. No identity-based campaign, no social movement can ever be as powerful as the working class. The global working class is, after all, counted in the billions.
- The working class has traditionally been organised politically by social democratic parties and economically by the trade unions. These organisations became integrated into the state. Social democracy does not threaten the state because it is an institution of the state. The unions do not threaten the state because they have become institutions of the state. Communist or socialist parties that cling to a belief in trade union paths to combat capitalism are "hoping" that they can move organisations that have long been co-opted into state institutions. It is a vain hope that can only end in tears. The working class has no capacity for independent action, because their institutions have

become state institutions.

- The only path for independent activity for the working class can be through a political party that seeks to challenge and replace capitalism. Capital is a global force. It does not recognise national borders. The working class, too, is a global class but is trapped into a perspective that is bound up in nationalist symbolism. A political struggle against a global enemy can, therefore, only be waged on a global battleground.

So, at the end of the day, the simple fact of the matter is that political organisation is at the very centre of Marxist approaches to political and economic change. It is necessary to arm the working class with a theory that will challenge capitalism. If you say it quickly it doesn't seem too hard but as we all can appreciate, it is a lot easier said than done, and especially so when the "marketplace" is cluttered with players laying claim to the Marxist mantle. These are the ideological battles that will be waged and are continually being waged. Things are becoming sharper, more acute and the cauldron of anxiety swirls with ever greater intensity. All of our futures demand that these battles be fought and won in order to resolve that other, bigger battle: the changing of the world.

Marxists are optimists. It is not the optimism of the wishful-thinker. It is based on a theory that is inherently optimistic. Earlier in this discussion the idea that Marx described his work as scientific was briefly described. It is in this context that Marxists remain optimistic. Lenin was quoted earlier in relation to how Marx studied the birth of a new society by examining what was happening to the old society. It is exactly the same today. Capitalism has nothing left to offer. It was once a progressive force that shaped a new world. Today it desperately clings to survival and seems prepared to destroy everything – people, society, the very planet – to maintain the thin grip it holds.

Recognising this fact, that capitalism is now past its use-by-date, is not difficult. The facts speak for themselves. It is possible to envisage a better world, one with a future, but that future must be striven for. If power is not taken out of the sclerotic hands of capitalism and its state, then the future is one of barbarism, war, desolation and fascism. This is a distinct possibility but need not be an inevitability. Change can only happen if it is made to happen. That is why Marxists maintain that an economic system based on exploitation must be replaced by a new economic system and that a moribund political system must be replaced by something better. It is not the dream of a utopian, never to be achieved future. It is an item on a far more immediate agenda and its immediacy is because the stakes are just too high to behave in any other way.

Chapter 8

Conclusion

Roberto, the character in *Down by Law*, whom we met at the beginning of the book, repeated, with what appeared to be an absurd optimism, that "it's a sad and beautiful world". Life for him was anything but "beautiful". In spite of the odds, life somehow worked out for Roberto, but it was more by luck, than good judgement. Trotsky, writing just months before his murder and after years in exile, remarked that "life is beautiful. Let the future generations cleanse it of all evil, oppression, and violence and enjoy it to the full" (Hallas 1970). Trotsky's optimism was the optimism of one who knew that there was something better and knew that it was achievable, but only achievable by arming the working class with a theory and practice that would enable it to change the world. That idea, that belief in the future, is what has framed the foregoing arguments. There is always a guiding factor above all others that motivates someone to sit down and write. Mine has been to offer a defence of an idea that is worth defending. It is by no means a complete or thorough defence. It merely points to paths that are worth travelling.

Reference was made to a basic element of the Marxist method of analysis. I did not go into exhaustive detail. It was not essential. I referred to how, in Marxist analysis, things are connected and interconnected and that to arbitrarily cherry-pick this or that issue in not so splendid isolation leads us nowhere. The connectivity of these themes remains central to the Marxist method of understanding and interpreting the world and how it turns. Marxism synthesises what are all too often resented as seemingly separate elements of capitalist relations, beginning with the role of labour and concluding with the development of globalisation. Marx (1974) argued that what was essential was to make observations that move from the simple to the complex and that show the inter-relationship of all component parts. In much the same way, we can observe the historical development of capitalism, from whence it came, of its progressive stage, its peak and decline into a regressive and destructive system; destructive of itself and all whose lives are ensnared by it. Capitalism has not always been. It is not an immutable, eternal force. It had a beginning, a middle and now we are witnessing what Trotsky so aptly described as its death agony.

The book has been structured with that progression, from the simple to the complex, in mind. The existential crisis of war and climate change is the end-point, but the crisis of capitalism in the twenty-first century is also about the "little things", the struggle by ordinary people to keep themselves well, housed and with some aspirations for their children. Their difficulties, our difficulties, appear in any manner of psychoses, that are caused by that same capitalism and which are being so woefully addressed, in the main, by the state. The end-point is only reached by a series of small things. Each painful and stressful step is an indictment of capitalism and of its incapacity to resolve any of its contradictions and crises, as it lurches towards its own end-point.

If truth be told, few will lament the eventual passing of capitalism. However, while many would be happy to see it gone, few have, until now, been prepared to hasten its demise. This, it has been shown, is because the capitalist state has so assiduously promoted the view that there is no alternative and certainly no better alternative. Marxism is that guiding influence that will help bring many to the realisation of the need to clear the decks and to give them the optimism that it can and must be done. We are not talking of a utopia, but of a set of objective realities. These realities are already acting to draw more and more people into conscious dispute with the state and capital.

Utopia and Dystopia

Marx wrote more than a little critically of utopian views of the world. After all they were, well, utopian and utopia, from the Greek, literally means "no place". Marx was conscious of working in and with the world as it was. Utopia, as a concept, first emerged in 1516 in Thomas More's work of the same name. Centuries later, William Morris, in a play on words, wrote his *News from Nowhere* (1890), which argued for a society that was as near to perfect as could be imagined. He took on board Marxist ideas. It was a work of optimism, as was that of his contemporary Edward Bellamy and his *Looking Backward* (1888) reflected the mood of the age. They were books that looked to a society that could be built and be free of exploitation and where people shared the wealth that they created. These writers had some cause for optimism. Capitalism was expanding and critics of capitalism saw a future without capitalist exploitation as being better than the present and an achievable future.

Popular fiction of the early twenty-first century is a million miles from those utopian visions. Dystopia has become the catch-cry. Dystopia, "bad place" in Greek, has all but become the norm. Themes of nuclear disaster, environmental destruction, technological control, survival and loss of individuality abound. If one word could sum up much of this writing, it is despair. The best that can be hoped for is to survive another day, a week, a month. The individual, alienated and apart, seeks survival in a desolate world. We've come a long way in the past century or so.

What is disturbing in such literature is that while the books and films are invariably set in a future, not always that far off, they are becoming less and less the work of science fiction. If we could step back in time, just a generation, or two at the most, it would be hard to find many who would accept a vision of a world where workers rights were routinely trampled upon, where working hours were growing, where wages were shrinking, where the social wage was being destroyed, where the age for pensions was being pushed out because the state claims that it cannot support an ageing population. It would be hard to get many to accept that with the end of the cold war, the threat of nuclear war was even more possible. It would be harder still to tell those children who sat huddled around television sets watching the moon landing that they would live to see the planet so visibly threatened by climate change. Things were meant to get better but then, within a very few short years, the hopes and aspirations of millions of ordinary, decent, hardworking men and women were turned to dust. That dystopian future, that popular fiction invokes is less and less fiction, less and less something for another time or age. We are living with such negative change as to make dystopia a creeping reality.

We are, of course, not characters in a work of fiction, but beings who can and must have choice, who can bring about a better future. It is, as Marx described, a situation whereby, "men make their own history, but they do not make it just as they please; they do not make it under circumstances chosen by themselves, but under circumstances directly encountered, given and transmitted from the past" (Marx 1986a: 97). It is in appreciating that simple fact that allows us the freedom to be optimistic. The people will make their own history and it will be made from the conditions they inherit. Those conditions in the twenty-first century include the astonishing accumulation of advances in science, technology and innovation that capitalism has brought to the world and which can be used for the betterment of the world, as well as that other and ever-present reality; destruction, anarchy and havoc that later capitalism has wrought.

The arguments that have framed this discussion have sought to portray capitalism's development and decay. The downward trajectory of capitalism is plain for all to see and is bound up with its inability to escape its own destructive set of contradictions that once drove it forward and now pull it towards an inevitable destruction. These contradictions include:

the private ownership of the means of production and the social nature of the production process; the drive to maximise profit by expanding the productive processes and surplus value, which necessitates limiting real wages growth; the imperative to increase labour productivity contributing to the tendency for profit rates to fall; and the drive to a globalised economy, while maintaining a system of nation-states. Any progressive role that capitalism might have had is long gone. What remains unchanged is its motivation for survival, regardless of the cost to the people or the planet. Decades ago, Trotsky described the future convulsions of capitalism as its death agony.

The death agony of capitalism

Cynics might point out that Trotsky wrote those words in 1938. They might say that its death is a long time coming. Since that time, capitalism rebounded and enjoyed its brief "golden age". It also brought us fascism and WWII with its death toll of 75 million. It has given us the threat of nuclear annihilation, deep economic recessions, the destruction of national economies, the endless war on terrorism, global interstate rivalries that again threaten our survival, a destruction of the environment that could, potentially, end human life, the return of fascistic ideas that reach to governmental levels and the impoverishment of countless millions, while at the same time obscene levels of wealth are gathered into the hands of so few. Capitalism's death agony might be a protracted one but it is clear for all to see and is having a devastating effect on us all.

Mankind's productive forces stagnate...conjunctural crises under the conditions of the social crisis of the whole capitalist system inflict ever heavier deprivations and sufferings... International relations present no better picture. Under the increasing tension of capitalist disintegration, imperialist antagonisms reach an impasse at the height of which separate clashes and bloody local disturbances...must inevitably coalesce into a conflagration of world dimensions (Trotsky 1977).

Those words were written in the 1930s, but it might as easily have been today. Such is the crisis that we are all facing. The quotation does, of course, focus on the big picture. In this sense it is at one with much that can be found in Marxist literature. It is the big brush approach. But, if we look closely, the canvas also includes those areas of minute detail that affect the day-to-day lives of ordinary people. These are the people being driven to despair by capitalism and caught up in its death agony. The physical and psychological effects of this can be seen in the deepening degree of alienation that is the product of late capitalism. The book highlighted the intensification of fear and anxiety that accompany this slow death of capitalism. It outlined why things must change and, to a degree, how people might prepare to change things.

The book paints a bleak picture, but not a picture of despair. It is a landscape that barely sustains life and yet is optimistic. Its optimism is not that of the Polyanna and nor is its portrayal of the desolation that accompanies capitalism a hopeless picture. Too many people, for too long, would "knowingly" declare that "things have got to get a lot worse yet". These were the dismal voices that seemingly wished for dark times that would shake the working class from its apathy. Today, it is the people, themselves, who are demanding something better. They are not prepared to wait for a day when things can't get any worse, because, unhappily, things can always get worse. On the contrary, the working class is beginning to discern a sense of its own power. It is an awareness that mis-leadership by those whose task it was to lead the class could not extinguish, just as those who sought so diligently to smother all vestiges of class awareness were, in the end, unsuccessful.

Fresh air and clear light

The book argued that alienation has become such a pervasive thing that it affects even those who appear to be waging battle against capitalism and its state. To this end, there was a brief exploration of the politics of identity, and social movement politics. These have become synonymous with anti-capitalist campaigns. However, as was shown, no matter how successful a campaign around the politics of identity might be, capitalism is not weakened by one iota. The campaigners gather people to their various banners, expend energies and can even, on occasion, claim victories but at the end of the day capital remains. The state apparatus will often use such identity campaigns to point to the health of a system that tolerates protest, accepts criticism and "listens" to the voice of the people. Activists come and activists go, sometimes in confusion, sometimes in exasperation, but ultimately, they go without challenging the system that they hoped and earnestly believed they were challenging.

It was also shown that by dint of hard work and persistence the state has been able to convince the mass of the people that we are all in this together, that we have more in common with "our" ruling class than with the interests of people very like ourselves in other countries. It has been a triumph of ideological control of a people; whether it be called false consciousness or cultural hegemony. As the crisis in capitalism deepened, the strategy of the state adapted. Nationalist symbolism and the call to patriotism became almost universal across the world. During the "golden age" of capitalism, this nationalist fervour had all but disappeared. After all, memories of its more negative consequences still resonated. It has only been in the past few decades that the state has felt it necessary to crank up the rhetoric to new heights. Today, there is a clarion call that populists and populist governments share; making "our" country great regales that it must come at the loss of "greatness" for someone else and the threat of war that goes with such calls. The book also noted a shift in thinking about the issue of populism. Where once it was recognised that populist ideologies threatened the *status quo*, there are more voices being raised that claim populism might be a "saviour" for capitalist democracy.

The book focused in its early chapters on how capitalism was destroying lives and of the devastation that increasing alienation brings. Fear, anxiety, impoverishment, both materially and spiritually, addiction, loss of self, the atomisation of society were all briefly detailed. There is an inescapable link between what some might see as the "small things" and the bigger issues of economic destruction, war and environmental catastrophe. All serve to make the individual even more alone and fearful. A brief overview, a checklist of the crises facing capitalism in the world, indicates the depth of the problem, of why the cauldron of anxiety is so fierce, but also why the future can be faced with optimism.

A checklist

This "checklist" is in no particular order of significance. Each has a direct impact on the next and forms a whole, which becomes a hole from which capitalism is unable to climb. This book was written in late 2019 and into 2020. The end of a decade allows for a look back and the view from the rear-view mirror is not very pleasant from the point of view of capitalism and its state. The decade began with the global economy still reeling from the 2008 financial crisis. These were years of extraordinary amounts of money going to bail out banks while government after government implemented austerity measures that had such a devastating effect on the lives of the working class in so many countries. Not surprisingly, it was the working class, the poor, the defenceless, that bore the brunt of capitalism's crisis.

Under such conditions, it is even less surprising to see a virtual breakdown of democratic institutions and to observe that the sense of legitimacy in the state has been shattered.

This, as has been shown, is not an exclusive problem of this or that country but is symptomatic of a crisis that can no longer be ignored. Anti-Semitism is rising alongside Islamophobia, racism and violence across all states. Mass shootings in the US set an unenviable record in 2019, but as it reflects a breakdown of the nation-state and of capitalist relations, then it will, in all likelihood, be a short-lived record.

None of that can be divorced from the militarisation of society and the state of perpetual war that has been waged now for decades and which cannot be stopped. Police forces in many countries more and more resemble the military. Tear gas and pepper spray is now synonymous with crowd control. Armoured vehicles and heavily-armed police are no longer uncommon sights on the streets of our cities.

While the cities are being militarised, war is unending. There was not one day in the decade just passed that the US and its closest allies were not at war. As this concluding chapter was being written, the US, by its killing of Iranian Major General Suleimani, pushed the world closer to an even more terrifying escalation of conflict. The influential International Institute for Strategic Studies' (IISS) annual Strategic Survey includes a "prospectives" chapter that looks at the future and particularly as it relates to the rise of China. Its estimation is that "for its part, the US is not likely voluntarily, reluctantly or after some sort of battle, to pass any strategic baton to China" (IISS 2019). It is not being alarmist to speak of the potential for nuclear war. It is being seriously considered. The same IISS report chillingly comments that "all that can be said with reasonable certainty is that a limited, regional nuclear exchange, under some circumstances, has severe global environmental effects. But under other circumstances, the effects could be minimal" (IISS 2019). The US is currently manufacturing "low-yield" nuclear weapons. Doubtless these are to produce that "minimal" effect on the environment.

The book closely linked the twin crises of war and its existential nature with that of environmental destruction and climate change. It made the point that war and environmental destruction have a common cause and that cause is capitalism. As the decade ended, there was effective consensus on the part of science and the people of the planet that things were spinning wildly out of control. Millions of people around the world have taken to the streets. The United Nations Climate Change Conference in Madrid ended, however, with little to show. Some governments are openly hostile to attempts to effect change. Others make appropriate noises, and some do as much as the economic system in which they operate allows. As the new decade dawned, the international media was tuned to the inferno that engulfed large parts of Australia. It was simply the latest in what will become an ongoing series of catastrophes. If nothing is done, then nothing will be able to be done. While the world burns, however, the grotesque fact remains that just 100 corporations are responsible for 71 per cent of carbon emissions. These same capitalist enterprises are rarely held to account. It is a final damnation of capitalism.

Central to the arguments that the book has presented is the appreciation that none of the above problems can be addressed while the system that created and exacerbates the problems remains intact. The arguments have been based on core elements of classical Marxist theory. This theory, in turn, is predicated on the idea that the working class is or can become the class that has the potential to challenge the *status quo*. This connection is what provides the sense of optimism that pervades this work. We have a crisis of unparalleled dimensions. We have a population that is living with uncertainty, with fear not only in the day-to-day realities of life, work and economic hardship, but with the knowledge that they share a planet that is under extreme threat, and yet there is hope, there is optimism, and it is all tied up with the theory that forms the basis for the book.

Creating a better future

It has been argued that the working class is the class with the capacity and potential to challenge capitalist rule. The term "revolutionary potential" was used. It was further shown why such a claim could be argued and three points were then raised to offer some proof of the statement. These points were: that the working class, by dint of its labour, produces and reproduces capitalist production, that the needs and aspirations of opposing classes in society are inevitably at variance with each other, and finally that the working class has become a globalised class as capitalism has become a globalised economic structure. The size of this globalised working class, today, makes up close to half of the world's population. There are fully 3.5 billion members of the working class. They have, ultimately, much more in common with each other, regardless of which continent they inhabit, than with the class that becomes rich from their labour. This is a simple statement of fact.

The growth of this class is the direct result of capitalism's need to expand and to pursue economic globalisation. Profits begin to fall and so, to maintain profit rates, capital is compelled to seek both new markets and new less expensive centres of manufacturing. The result is that capitalism has now reached every corner of the planet and consequently we have a working class that is 3.5 billion-strong. This potentially powerful class has been kept in a fog of confusion and kept from appreciating its very real power. How much longer the state apparatus of each nation can hope to maintain this power through confusion, is a moot point.

Looking back over the decade that was ending as this book was being written, was revealing and offers a view that must be disquieting for capitalism. Mass demonstrations and strikes erupted all over the world. There were significant movements of worker unrest in Mexico, Puerto Rico, Ecuador, Colombia, Chile, France, Spain, Algeria, Britain, Lebanon, Iraq, Iran, Kenya, South

Africa and India. In the heartland of capitalist power, the US, there were strikes, the size of which had not been witnessed for decades. In China, the alleged socialist state was regularly repressing workers strikes.

Where only a few years ago the working class acted purely within the domain of their own country, they are increasingly recognising the commonality of their grievances and the common enemy that they are confronting. Climate change actions have been organised across continents, and there have been expressions of solidarity between workers across states. These all give evidence, if in early stages of formation, of a change in perceptions. The question for Marxists has always been and remains, the question of leadership. As the book emphasised, no degree of wanting, or wishing, or expressed solidarity, or heroism, can be expected to prevail without there being a leadership that can draw these forces into action and draw them into action around a programme that can work. This can only be expressed through the auspices of a political organisation and given the internationalism of the working class and the globalisation of capitalism, that political expression needs to be similarly global in its approach and organisation. This remains a task that appears to be a daunting one but, if the premise of the book is to be considered seriously, then it is a task that needs not only to be considered but attempted.

The book began with one basic premise, from which a range of ideas and arguments flowed. It was stated that it was a defence of an idea that was worth defending. That idea, Marxism, has been defended, albeit in an abbreviated manner, but the book was never to be a book just about Marxist theory. Shelves already groan under the weight of often conflicting "Marxist" theories. It also sought to juggle two seemingly contradictory concepts. It outlined the bleak present and potentially disastrous future that capitalism offers the world, the dystopia that stalks the planet. It also maintained an air of optimism and that, while existential crises of capitalism were imminent, they were not unavoidable. After all, as the quotation, allegedly by Lenin, has it, "there are decades where nothing happens; and there are weeks where decades happen".

And so, the cauldron of capitalist anxiety swirls and bubbles. It is fraught with danger. It can drown us all, or we can extinguish the fire that makes it bubble so ferociously. As Marx so eloquently put it, philosophers have only interpreted the world, in various ways; the point is to change it. This little book is but a tiny step in that direction.

Bibliography

Acemoglu, D and Robinson, J 2019, "The Upside of Populism", *Foreign Policy*, Retrieved 26 November 2019, https://foreignpolicy.com/2019/10/19/populism-us-democracy-trump/

Appleton, J 2019, "Self, Society, Alienation: From Marx to Identity Politics" in A Kennedy & J Panton (eds) *From Self to Selfie: a critique of contemporary forms of alienation*, Palgrave Macmillan, Cham Switzerland: 129-146

Anselmi, M 2017, *Populism: An Introduction*, Routledge, Oxon & New York

Ayres, JM 2001, "Transnational Political Processes and Contention Against the Global Economy", *Mobilization: An International Quarterly*, vol. 6, no.1 Spring: 55-68

Bello, W 2013, *Capitalism's Last Stand: Deglobalization in the Age of Austerity*, Zed Books

Bernanke, BS 2006, *Global Economic Integration: What's New and What's Not?* Speech at the Federal Reserve Bank of Kansas City's Thirtieth Annual Economic Symposium, Jackson Hole, Wyoming, Retrieved 23 November 2019, https://www.federalreserve.gov/newsevents/speech/bernanke20060825a.htm

Borger, J 2019, "US Nuclear Weapons: first low-yield warheads roll off the production line" *The Guardian*, 28 January 2019, Retrieved 20 December, 2019, https://www.theguardian.com/world/2019/jan/28/us-nuclear-weapons-first-low-yield-warheads-roll-off-the-production-line

Boyd, S 2019, "How Chile Went From an Economic Star to an Angry Mess", *The Washington Post*, 24 October, 2019, Retrieved 22 November 2019, https://www.washingtonpost.com/business/how-chile-went-from-an-economic-star-to-an-angry-mess/2019/10/29/9d575fe8-fa41-11e9-9e02-

1d45cb3dfa8f_story.html

Bruce, C 2014, "Green Anarchy: Towards the Abolition of Hierarchy", *Anarchist News*, 30 August 2014, Retrieved 20 December 2019, https://ecology.iww.org/node/743?bot_test=1

Burgoon, B 2013 "Inequality and anti-globalization backlash by political parties" *European Union Politics*, vol. 14, no. 3: 498-435

Burns, AF 1969, "Progress Towards Economic Stability" in AF Burns (ed) *The Business Cycle in a Changing World, National Bureau of Economic Research,* Cambridge Massachusetts: 101-128

Burston, D 2014, "Cyborgs, Zombies and Planetary Death", *The Humanistic Psychologist*, vol. 42, no. 3: 283-291

Castells, M 2004, *The Power of Identity: The Information Age: Economy, Society and Culture Volume 2,* 2nd edn Wiley & Blackwell, Malden MA, Oxford, Chichester, UK

Colby, E 2018, "If You Want Peace, Prepare for Nuclear War: A Strategy for the New Great-Power Rivalry", *Foreign Affairs*, November/December 2018, Retrieved 20 December, 2019, https://www.foreignaffairs.com/articles/china/2018-10-15/if-you-want-peace-prepare-nuclear-war

Collier, P 2018, *The Future of Capitalism: Facing the New Anxieties,* Harper Collins Publishers, New York

Cox, RW 1993, "Gramsci, Hegemony and International Relations: An Essay in Method", in S Gill (ed), *Gramsci, Historical Materialism and International Relations,* Cambridge University Press: 49-66

Credit Suisse 2015, *Global Wealth Report 2015,* Credit Suisse Research Institute, Retrieved 23 July 2019 http://www.protothema.gr/files/1/2015/10/14/ekthsi_0.pdf

Crenshaw, K 1993, *Mapping the Margins: Intersectionality, Identity Politics, and Violence Against Women of Color,* Retrieved 15 November 2019, http://socialdifference.columbia.edu/files/socialdiff/projects/Article__Mapping_the_Margins_by_

Kimblere_Crenshaw.pdf

Cushman, JH 2016, "Warren Buffett Delivers Cold-Blooded View of Global Warming to Shareholders", *Inside Climate News*, 29 February 2016, Retrieved 14 January 2020, https://insideclimatenews.org/news/29022016/warren-buffett-tells-shareholders-climate-change-not-entirely-bad-business-berkshire-hathaway-insurance

Dabla, E, Kochhar, K, Suphaphiphat, N Ricka F and Tsounta, E 2015, "Causes and Consequences of Income Inequality: A Global Perspective", *IMF Strategy, Policy and Review Department*, Retrieved 20 July 2019 https://www.imf.org/external/pubs/ft/sdn/2015/sdn1513.pdf

Dallmayr, FR 2002, "Globalization and Inequality: A Plea For Global Justice", International Studies Review, vol. 4, no. 2: 137-156

Deutsche Welle 2019, "What's behind the protests in Iraq?" Deutsche Welle, 5 October, 2019, Retrieved 23 November 2019, https://www.dw.com/en/whats-behind-the-protests-in-iraq/a-50712024

Deutscher, I 1973, edited by T Deutscher *Marxism in our Time*, Ramparts Press, San Francisco

Dobbs, R Madgavkar, A, Barton, D, Labaye, E, Manyoka, J, Roxburgh, C, Lund, S and Madhav, S 2012, "The World at Work, Jobs, pay and skills for 3.5 billion people", *McKinsey Global Institute*, McKinsey and Company, Retrieved, 22 November 2019, http://www.mckinsey.com/global-themes/employment-and-growth/the-world-at-work

Engels, F 1984, *The Condition of the Working Class in England*, Progress Publishers, Moscow & Lawrence & Wishart, London

Engels, F 1986, *Socialism: Utopian and Scientific*, in Marx Engels: Selected Works Progress Publishers, Moscow: 375-428

Engels, F 2000, "A Letter to Franz Mehring" Retrieved 5 August 2019, *Marx-Engels Correspondence 1893*, http://www.marxists.org/archive/marx/works/1893/letters/93_07_14.htm

Forbes, S and Ames, E 2009, *How Capitalism Will Save US: why free people and free markets are the best answer in today's economy*, Crown Publishing, New York

Franklin, B 1997, *Newszak and News Media*, Arnold, London

FRED 2013, Personal Consumption Expenditures – FRED Graph, Federal Reserve Bank of St Louis, retrieved 30 October 2019 https://research.stlouisfed.org/

Fuentes-Ramirez, RR 2014, "Marxist Perspectives on Twenty-first Century Transition to Socialism", *Socialism and Democracy*, vol. 28 no. 1: 123-142

Gamble, A 1999, "Marxism after Communism: Beyond Realism and Historicism", *Review of International Studies*, vol. 25 The Interregnum: Controversies in World Politics 1989-1999: 127-144

Gilley, B 2006, "The Meaning and Measure of State Legitimacy: Results for 72 Countries", *European Journal of Political Research*, vol. 45, no. 3: 499-525

Gilpin, RG 2000, *The Challenge of Global Capitalism: The World Economy in the 21st Century*, Princeton University Press

Goodwin and J Jasper (Eds) 2009, *Rethinking Social Movements: Structure, Meaning, and Emotion*, Lanham, MD: Rowman & Littlefield, Lanham, MD: 135-154

Gordon, RG 2016, *The Rise and Fall of American Growth: the US standard of living since the Civil War*, Princeton University Press, Princeton US

Gray, J 2002, *False Dawn: The Delusion of Global Capitalism*, Granta Books, London

Grier, P 2005, "Rich-Poor Gap Gaining Attention", *Christian Science Monitor*, Washington

Griffith, P 2017 CDP Carbon Majors Report, Carbon Majors Database, Retrieved 11 November 2019, https://b8f65cb373b1b7b15feb-c70d8ead6ced550b4d987d7c03fcdd1d.ssl.cf3.rackcdn.com/cms/reports/documents/000/002/327/original/Carbon-Majors-Report-2017.pdf

Guigni, M 1999, "Introduction: How Social Movements Matter: Past Research, Present Problems, Future Developments", in M Guigni, D McAdam, C Tilly (eds) *How Social Movements Matter*, University of Minnesota Press: xii-xxxiii

H. Res.109 2019, "Recognizing the duty of the Federal Government to create a green new deal", *Congress.Gov*, Retrieved, 22 December 2019 https://www.congress.gov/bill/116th-congress/house-resolution/109

Hallas, D 1970, "Trotsky", *Marxist Internet Archive*, Retrieved 28 January 2020, https://www.marxists.org/archive/hallas/works/1970/08/trotsky.htm

Harman, C 1991, "The State and Capitalism Today", *International Socialism*, Summer 1991: 3-54

Harvey, D 2012, *Rebel Cities: From the Right to the City to the Urban Revolution*, Verso, London and New York

Hay, C 1999, "Marxism and the State", in A Gamble, D Marsh and T Tant (eds) *Marxism and Social Science*, University of Illinois Press, Urbana and Chicago

Hay, P 2002, *Main Currents in Western Environmental Thought*, UNSW Press Sydney

Horner, R, Schindler, S, Haberly, D and Aoyama, Y 2018 "Globalisation, uneven development and the North-South 'big switch'", *Cambridge Journal of Regions, Economy and Society*, vol. 11, no. 1: 17-33

IISS 2019, "Prospectives", *Strategic Survey Journal* 2019, vol. 119, no. 1: 11-18

Ignatow, G 2007, *Transnational Identity Politics and the Environment*, Lexington Books, a division of Rowman & Littlefield Inc., Lanham, Boulder, New York, Toronto, Plymouth UK

International Labour Office, 2008, *Global Wage Report*, Retrieved 13 November 2019 http://www.ilo.org/wcmsp5

Kaska, PB 2007, "Militarization and Policing – Its Relevance to 21st Century Police", *Policing: A Journal of Policy and Practice*, vol.1 no. 4: 501-513

Kauffman, LA 2001, "The Anti-Politics of Identity" in B Ryan (ed) *Identity Politics in the Women's Movement,* New York University Press, New York; 23-34

Klebnikov, S 2019, "Stopping Global Warming Will Cost $50 Trillion: Morgan Stanley Report", *Forbes* Retrieved 23 December 2019, https://www.forbes.com/sites/sergei klebnikov/2019/10/24/stopping-global-warming-will-cost-50-trillion-morgan-stanley-report/#589869eb51e2

Klein, N 2019, *On Fire: The Burning Case for a Green New Deal,* Allen Lane, London UK

Kyle, J and Gultchin, L 2019, Populists in Power Around the World, Tony Blair Institute for Global Change, Retrieved 25 November 2019, https://institute.global/insight/renewing-centre/populists-power-around-world

Laclau, E and Mouffe, C 2001 *Hegemony and Socialist Strategy: Towards a Radical Democratic Politics,* (2nd edn) Verso, London and New York

Lebowitz, MA 2004, "What Keeps Capitalism Going?" *Monthly Review,* vol.56, no. 2: 19-25

Lebowitz, MA 2013, "The Relevance of Marxism Today: An Interview with Michael A. Lebowitz by Zhuo Mingliang", *MRZine* 21 03 2013, Retrieved 30 September 2019, http://mrzine.monthlyreview.org/2013/lebowitz210313.html

Lenin, VI 1977, "The State and Revolution", *Lenin Selected Works, Volume 2,* Progress Publishers, Moscow: 238-327

Lukacs, G 1976, *History and Class Consciousness: Studies in Marxist Dialectics,* MIT Press, Cambridge Mass.

Luxemburg, R 2008, "The Junius Pamphlet: The Crisis of German Social Democracy", *Luxemburg Internet Archive,* Retrieved 10 December, 2019 https://www.marxists.org/archive/luxemburg/1915/junius/ch01.htm

Macionis, JJ 2007, *Sociology* 11th edn., Pearson/Prentice Hall, New Jersey

Marx, K and Engels, F 1964, *The German Ideology,* Progress

Publishers, Moscow

Marx, K 1974, *Grundrisse: Foundations of the Critique of Political Economy (Rough Draft)* Penguin Books, Harmondsworth, Middlesex, England

Marx, K 1984, *The Economic and Philosophic Manuscripts of 1844* International Publishers, New York

Marx, K 1986a, "The Eighteenth Brumaire of Louis Bonaparte", *in Marx Engels Selected Works*, Progress Publishers, Moscow: 94-117

Marx, K 1986b, *Capital: A Critique of Political Economy, Volume 1,* Progress Publishers, Moscow

Marx, K and Engels, F 1975, *The Holy Family: Critique of Critical Critique*, Progress Publishers, Moscow

Marx, K and Engels, F 1977, *Manifesto of the Communist Party*, Progress Publishers, Moscow

McAfee, A 2019, *More From Less: the surprising story of how we learned to prosper using fewer resources and what happens next*, Simon & Schuster, London, New York, Sydney, Toronto, New Delhi

McDonald, M, Wearing, S and Ponting, J 2007, "Narcissism and Neo-Liberalism: Work, Leisure, and Alienation in an Era of Consumption", *Loisir et Société/Society and Leisure*, vol. 30 no. 2: 489-510

McKnight, D 2018, *Populism Now!* Newsouth Publishing, Sydney, Australia

McPhee, P 2019, "In a world of upheaval, why aren't today's protests leading to revolutions?" *The Conversation*, 21 November 2019, Retrieved 22 November, 2019, https://theconversation.com/we-live-in-a-world-of-upheaval-so-why-arent-todays-protests-leading-to-revolutions-126505

Mental Health Foundation 2019, "Body Image: How we think and feel about our bodies", Mental Health Foundation London, retrieved 2 November 2019, https://www.mentalhealth.org.uk/publications/body-image-report

Miller, RW 1991, "Social and political theory: Class, state, revolution", in T Carver (ed) *The Cambridge Companion to Marx*, Cambridge University Press, Cambridge: 55-105

Mudde, C 2004, "The Populist Zeitgeist", *Government and Opposition*, No. 39, vol. 4: 542-563

Mudde, C and Kaaltwasser, C 2017, *Populism: A Very Short Introduction, Oxford University Press*

Muller, J-W, 2016, *What is Populism?* University of Pennsylvania, Philadelphia

National Institute for Occupational Safety and Health, 1999 Stress at Work, retrieved October 25, 2019 https://www.stress.org/workplace-stress

OECD 2019, *Suicide Rates* (indicator doi: 10.1787/a82f3459-en), retrieved October 27 2019 retrieved October 28, 2019 https://www.oecd-ilibrary.org/social-issues-migration-health/suicide-rates/indicator/english_a82f3459-en

OECD 2019, *Under Pressure: The Squeezed Middle Class*, OECD Publishing, Paris, https://doi.org/10.1787/689afed1-en

Orwell, G 1968, "Politics and the English Language", in S Orwell and I Angus (eds) *The Collected Essays, Journalism and Letters of George Orwell*, Harcourt, New York: 127-140

Oxfam 2018, *5 shocking facts about extreme global inequality and how to even it up*, Oxfam International, Retrieved 20 November 2019, https://www.oxfam.org/en/5-shocking-facts-about-extreme-global-inequality-and-how-even-it

Parents at Work 2019, *National Working Families Report 2019* retrieved 29 October 2019, www.parentsandcarersatwork.com/aplen

Pateman, C 1988, *The Sexual Contract*, Polity Press, Cambridge UK

Pieterse, JN 2002, "Global Inequality: bringing politics back in", *Third World Quarterly*, vol. 23, no. 6: 1023-1046

Piven FF 1995, "Globalizing Capitalism and the Rise of Identity Politics" *Socialist Register*, vol. 31: 102-116

Plescia, C, Kritzinger S and De Sio, L 2019, "Filling the Void? Political Responsiveness of Populist Parties", *Representation*, Retrieved 27 November 2019 DOI: 10.1080/00344893.2019.1635197

Rees, J 1998, *The Algebra of Revolution: The Dialectic and the Classical Marxist Tradition*, Routledge, London & New York

Reveley, J 2013, "Understanding Social Media Use as Alienation: a review and antique", E-Learning and Digital Media, vol. 10, no. 1: 83-94

Rodrik, D 1997, *Has Globalization Gone Too Far?* Institute for International Economics, Washington DC

Rootes, CA 1997, "Social movements and politics", *African Studies*, vol. 56 no. 1: 67-95

Schor J 1993, *The Overworked American: the unexpected decline of leisure*, Basic Books, New York

Schulzke, M 2017, "Necessary and surplus militarisation: Rethinking civil-military interactions and their consequences", *European Journal of International Security*, vol. 3 no.1: 94-112

Sklair, L 2002, *Globalization: Capitalism & its Alternatives*, 3rd edn, Oxford University Press

Smith, S 1994, "Mistaken identity: or can identity politics liberate the oppressed?" *International Socialism Journal* vol. 62, Spring 1994

Smith, J 2001, "Globalizing Resistance: The Battle of Seattle and the Future of Social Movements", *Mobilization: An International Quarterly*, vol. 6, no. 1 Spring: 1-20

Stiglitz, JE 2006, *Making Globalization Work*, WW Norton & Co., New York, London

Stoker, G, Evans, M and Halupka, M 2018, "Trust and Democracy in Australia", *Democracy 2025*, Retrieved 17 November 2019, https://www.democracy2025.gov.au/documents/Democracy2025-report1.pdf

Temple, M 2006, "Dumbing Down is Good for You", *British Politics*, vol.1: 257-273

Therborn, G 2012, "Class in the 21st Century", *New Left Review*, vol. 78

Tormey, S 2019, *Populism: A Beginner's Guide*, Oneworld Publications, London UK

Trotsky, L 1956, "Nationalism and International Life", *Fourth International*, vol. 17, no. 2: 18-21

Trotsky, LD 1965, *The History of the Russian Revolution, Volume One*, translated from the Russian by Max Eastman, Sphere Books Limited, London

Trotsky, L 1971, *In Defense of Marxism*, New Park Publications, London

Trotsky, L 1972, *On Marxism and the Trade Unions: Trade unions in the epoch of imperialist decay*, New Park Publications, London

Trotsky, L 1977, *The Transitional Programme for Socialist Revolution*, Pathfinder Press, New York

Victims of Communism Memorial Foundation 2019, "US Attitudes Toward Socialism, Communism, and Collectivism".

Walker, D 2015, "Towards a New Gospel of Wealth" Ford Foundation, Retrieved 2 November 2019, https://www.fordfoundation.org/ideas/equals-change-blog/posts/toward-a-new-gospel-of-wealth/

Wheelwright, EL 1953, "Trade Unions and the State", *The Australian Quarterly*, vol. 25, no. 2: 26-36

Wike, R, Silver, L and Castillo, A 2019, "Many Across the Globe are Dissatisfied with How Democracy is Working", Pew Research Center, Retrieved 15 November 2019, https://www.pewresearch.org/global/2019/04/29/many-across-the-globe-are-dissatisfied-with-how-democracy-is-working/

Wolf, M 2004, *Why Globalization Works*, Yale University Press, New Haven Connecticut

WMO 2019, "Greenhouse gas concentrations in atmosphere reach another high", *World Meteorological Organization*, Retrieved 20 December 2019, https://public.wmo.int/en/media/press-release/greenhouse-gas-concentrations-atmosphere-reach-yet-another-high

World Trade Organisation, 2016 *Report on G20 Trade Measures (mid-October 2015 to mid-May 2016)* WTO-OMC, Retrieved 22 November 2019 https://www.wto.org/english/news_e/ news16_e/g20_wto_report_june16_e.pdf

Zimbalist, A and Sherman, HJ 1984, *Comparing Economic Systems: a political-economic approach,* Academic Press Inc., Orlando Florida

CULTURE, SOCIETY & POLITICS

The modern world is at an impasse. Disasters scroll across our smartphone screens and we're invited to like, follow or upvote, but critical thinking is harder and harder to find. Rather than connecting us in common struggle and debate, the internet has sped up and deepened a long-standing process of alienation and atomization. Zer0 Books wants to work against this trend. With critical theory as our jumping off point, we aim to publish books that make our readers uncomfortable. We want to move beyond received opinions.

Zer0 Books is on the left and wants to reinvent the left. We are sick of the injustice, the suffering and the stupidity that defines both our political and cultural world, and we aim to find a new foundation for a new struggle.

If this book has helped you to clarify an idea, solve a problem or extend your knowledge, you may want to check out our online content as well. Look for Zer0 Books: Advancing Conversations in the iTunes directory and for our Zer0 Books YouTube channel.

Popular videos include:

Žižek and the Double Blackmain

The Intellectual Dark Web is a Bad Sign

Can there be an Anti-SJW Left?

Answering Jordan Peterson on Marxism

Follow us on Facebook
at https://www.facebook.com/ZeroBooks and Twitter at https://twitter.com/Zer0Books

Bestsellers from Zer0 Books include:

Give Them An Argument
Logic for the Left
Ben Burgis
Many serious leftists have learned to distrust talk of logic. This is a serious mistake.
Paperback: 978-1-78904-210-8 ebook: 978-1-78904-211-5

Poor but Sexy
Culture Clashes in Europe East and West
Agata Pyzik
How the East stayed East and the West stayed West.
Paperback: 978-1-78099-394-2 ebook: 978-1-78099-395-9

An Anthropology of Nothing in Particular
Martin Demant Frederiksen
A journey into the social lives of meaninglessness.
Paperback: 978-1-78535-699-5 ebook: 978-1-78535-700-8

In the Dust of This Planet
Horror of Philosophy vol. 1
Eugene Thacker
In the first of a series of three books on the Horror of Philosophy,
In the Dust of This Planet offers the genre of horror as a way of
thinking about the unthinkable.
Paperback: 978-1-84694-676-9 ebook: 978-1-78099-010-1

The End of Oulipo?
An Attempt to Exhaust a Movement
Lauren Elkin, Veronica Esposito
Paperback: 978-1-78099-655-4 ebook: 978-1-78099-656-1

Capitalist Realism
Is There No Alternative?
Mark Fisher
An analysis of the ways in which capitalism has presented itself
as the only realistic political-economic system.
Paperback: 978-1-84694-317-1 ebook: 978-1-78099-734-6

Rebel Rebel
Chris O'Leary
David Bowie: every single song. Everything you want to know,
everything you didn't know.
Paperback: 978-1-78099-244-0 ebook: 978-1-78099-713-1

Kill All Normies
Angela Nagle
Online culture wars from 4chan and Tumblr to Trump.
Paperback: 978-1- 78535-543-1 ebook: 978-1-78535-544-8

Romeo and Juliet in Palestine
Teaching Under Occupation
Tom Sperlinger
Life in the West Bank, the nature of pedagogy and the role of a
university under occupation.
Paperback: 978-1-78279-637-4 ebook: 978-1-78279-636-7

Ghosts of My Life
Writings on Depression, Hauntology and Lost Futures
Mark Fisher
Paperback: 978-1-78099-226-6 ebook: 978-1-78279-624-4

Sweetening the Pill
or How We Got Hooked on Hormonal Birth Control
Holly Grigg-Spall
Has contraception liberated or oppressed women?
Sweetening the Pill breaks the silence on the dark side of hormonal
contraception.
Paperback: 978-1-78099-607-3 ebook: 978-1-78099-608-0

Why Are We The Good Guys?
Reclaiming your Mind from the Delusions of Propaganda
David Cromwell
A provocative challenge to the standard ideology that Western
power is a benevolent force in the world.
Paperback: 978-1-78099-365-2 ebook: 978-1-78099-366-9

The Writing on the Wall
On the Decomposition of Capitalism and its Critics
Anselm Jappe, Alastair Hemmens
A new approach to the meaning of social emancipation.
Paperback: 978-1-78535-581-3 ebook: 978-1-78535-582-0

Enjoying It
Candy Crush and Capitalism
Alfie Bown
A study of enjoyment and of the enjoyment of studying. Bown asks what enjoyment says about us and what we say about enjoyment, and why.
Paperback: 978-1-78535-155-6 ebook: 978-1-78535-156-3

Color, Facture, Art and Design
Iona Singh
This materialist definition of fine-art develops guidelines for architecture, design, cultural-studies and ultimately social change.
Paperback: 978-1-78099-629-5 ebook: 978-1-78099-630-1

Neglected or Misunderstood
The Radical Feminism of Shulamith Firestone
Victoria Margree
An interrogation of issues surrounding gender, biology, sexuality, work and technology, and the ways in which our imaginations continue to be in thrall to ideologies of maternity and the nuclear family.
Paperback: 978-1-78535-539-4 ebook: 978-1-78535-540-0

How to Dismantle the NHS in 10 Easy Steps (Second Edition)
Youssef El-Gingihy
The story of how your NHS was sold off and why you will have to buy private health insurance soon. A new expanded second edition with chapters on junior doctors' strikes and government blueprints for US-style healthcare.
Paperback: 978-1-78904-178-1 ebook: 978-1-78904-179-8

Digesting Recipes
The Art of Culinary Notation
Susannah Worth
A recipe is an instruction, the imperative tone of the expert, but
this constraint can offer its own kind of potential. A recipe need
not be a domestic trap but might instead offer escape – something
to fantasise about or aspire to.
Paperback: 978-1-78279-860-6 ebook: 978-1-78279-859-0

Most titles are published in paperback'and as an ebook.
Paperbacks are available in traditional bookshops. Both print and
ebook formats are available online.
Follow us on Facebook
at https://www.facebook.com/ZeroBooks
and Twitter at https://twitter.com/Zer0Books